A
—
JANE AUSTEN YEAR

A
JANE AUSTEN YEAR

JANE AUSTEN'S
HOUSE

PITKIN

CONTENTS

Introduction   6

January   10

February   28

March   44

April   60

May   76

June   92

July   108

August   124

September   140

October   156

November   172

December   188

Index   204
About Jane Austen's House   206
Picture credits   207

INTRODUCTION

This book is written from Jane Austen's House in Chawton – one of the most important places in the history of English literature and the development of the novel.

Here, in this inspiring Hampshire cottage, Jane Austen lived for the last eight years of her life. Here, her genius flourished and she wrote, revised and had published all six of her globally beloved novels: *Sense and Sensibility*, *Pride and Prejudice*, *Mansfield Park*, *Emma*, *Northanger Abbey* and *Persuasion*.

Today, Jane Austen's House is a cherished museum with an unparalleled collection of Austen treasures, including items of furniture, paintings and household objects. Visitors can discover Jane's personal letters and first editions of her novels, items of jewellery, portraits of her friends and family, and the tiny writing table at which she wrote.

This book brings together some of the precious fragments of Jane Austen's life story, along with world events that shaped her life and understanding, extracts from her novels and letters, and a range of extraordinary objects held here in the museum's collection. Dip into it as you will, or go through month by month and enjoy a full year of Jane Austen: her life and writings, people and objects she knew and, of course, her beautiful, inspiring home.

'Hitherto the weather
has been just what
we could wish;—the
continuance of the
dry Season is very
necessary to our
comfort.'

JANE TO CASSANDRA,
FRIDAY 14 SEPTEMBER 1804

8

JANUARY

In January 1776, when Jane was just a few weeks old, the Hampshire naturalist Gilbert White described the winter weather in his diary:

'January 7th. — Snow driving all day, which was followed by frost, sleet, and some snow, till the 12th, when a prodigious mass overwhelmed all the works of men, drifting over the tops of the gates and filling the hollow lanes.'

A TRIP TO LONDON

Jane Austen is famously precise about dates in her novels. In Sense and Sensibility, *the Dashwood sisters' trip to London takes place 'in the first week in January' – just at the start of the London Season.*

They were three days on their journey, and Marianne's behaviour as they travelled was a happy specimen of what future complaisance and companionableness to Mrs. Jennings might be expected to be. She sat in silence almost all the way, wrapt in her own meditations, and scarcely ever voluntarily speaking, except when any object of picturesque beauty within their view drew from her an exclamation of delight exclusively addressed to her sister. To atone for this conduct therefore, Elinor took immediate possession of the post of civility which she had assigned herself, behaved with the greatest attention to Mrs. Jennings, talked with her, laughed with her, and listened to her whenever she could; and Mrs. Jennings on her side treated them both with all possible kindness, was solicitous on every occasion for their ease and enjoyment, and only disturbed that she could not make them choose their own dinners at the inn, nor extort a confession of their preferring salmon to cod, or boiled fowls to veal cutlets. They reached town by three o'clock the third day, glad to be released, after such a journey, from the confinement of a carriage, and ready to enjoy all the luxury of a good fire.

The house was handsome, and handsomely fitted up, and the young ladies were immediately put in possession of a very comfortable apartment. It had formerly been Charlotte's, and over the mantelpiece still hung a landscape in coloured silks of her performance, in proof of her having spent seven years at a great school in town to some effect.

As dinner was not to be ready in less than two hours from their arrival, Elinor determined to employ the interval in writing to her mother, and sat down for that purpose. In a few moments Marianne did the same. 'I am writing home, Marianne,' said Elinor; 'had not you better defer your letter for a day or two?'

'I am not going to write to my mother,' replied Marianne, hastily, and as if wishing to avoid any farther inquiry. Elinor said no more; it immediately struck her that she must then be writing to Willoughby; and the conclusion which as instantly followed was, that, however mysteriously they might wish to conduct the affair, they must be engaged. This conviction, though not entirely satisfactory, gave her pleasure, and she continued her letter with greater alacrity. Marianne's was finished in a very few minutes; in length it could be no more than a note; it was then folded up, sealed, and directed with eager rapidity. Elinor thought she could distinguish a large W in the direction; and no sooner was it complete than Marianne, ringing the bell, requested the footman who answered it to get that letter conveyed for her to the two-penny post. This decided the matter at once.

SENSE AND SENSIBILITY, VOLUME II, CHAPTER 4

Illustration by Hugh Thomson for *Sense and Sensibility* (MacMillan & Co, 1896).

'To be fond of dancing
was a certain step
towards falling in love.'

PRIDE AND PREJUDICE,
VOLUME I, CHAPTER 3

DANCING WITH TOM LEFROY

In January 1796, when she had just turned 20, Jane Austen met Tom Lefroy, a clever young Irishman who had moved to London to study the law. He was staying with his uncle and aunt for the Christmas holidays, near to the Austen's home in Steventon, Hampshire.

Jane and Tom met frequently at Christmas balls and parties, where they danced, chatted and flirted. Jane described their behaviour in a letter to her sister Cassandra as 'everything most profligate and shocking in the way of dancing and sitting down together.'

They certainly enjoyed each other's company, but if Jane had hopes of marriage she was to be disappointed. Tom went back to London to resume his studies and Jane wrote to her sister:

'At length the Day is come on which I am to flirt my last with Tom Lefroy, & when you receive this it will be over— My tears flow as I write, at the melancholy idea.'

Some biographers have taken this at face value and assumed that she was really heartbroken, but it seems more likely that she was teasing Cassandra, in her usual style, and that the tears she mentions were no more than a twinkle in her eye.

After all, Jane was a realist. She might be a romantic in her novels, arguing for mutual love in marriage, but she was also practical and knew how essential a good income was to domestic happiness. Neither Tom nor Jane had the money to make a match possible.

And while Tom went back to work, Jane did too – in the autumn of 1796 she began writing *First Impressions*, published years later as *Pride and Prejudice*. It has been suggested that her romance with Tom may have inspired her to create the character of Mr Darcy, but again this doesn't seem right. Darcy is cold, arrogant and aloof – Tom Lefroy was amiable and fun – more like Mr Bingley than his proud friend.

Portrait miniature
of Tom Lefroy
by George
Engleheart, 1798.

PUBLICATION OF *PRIDE AND PREJUDICE*

Jane first drafted *Pride and Prejudice* in 1796, at her childhood home of Steventon Rectory. At this time the novel was called *First Impressions* and is thought to have been written as a series of letters.

When Jane arrived in Chawton in 1809, she took out her early manuscripts and set to work rewriting them for publication. First, she revised *Sense and Sensibility* and then she turned her attention to *First Impressions*, revising the manuscript extensively and giving it a new title.

Encouraged by the success of *Sense and Sensibility*, Jane's publisher Thomas Egerton, agreed to publish *Pride and Prejudice* at his own risk, by purchasing the copyright. Jane wrote to her friend Martha Lloyd:

'P. & P. is sold.—Egerton gives £110 for it.—I would rather have had £150, but we could not both be pleased, & I am not at all surprised that he should not chuse to hazard, so much.'

Pride and Prejudice was published on 28 January 1813. It sold well – the first edition (probably around 1500 copies) sold out quickly and became one of the most fashionable novels of the season.

According to Jane's brother Henry, the playwright Richard Sheridan called it 'one of the cleverest things he ever read', while another literary acquaintance assured Henry that it was 'much too clever to have been written by a woman'.

Jane herself was more critical, writing to Cassandra:

'The work is rather too light & bright & sparkling;—it wants shade;—it wants to be stretched out here & there with a long Chapter—of sense if it could be had, if not of solemn specious nonsense—about something unconnected with the story; an Essay on Writing, a critique on Walter Scott, or the history of Buonaparté—or anything that would form a contrast & bring the reader with increased delight to the playfulness & Epigrammatism of the general stile…'

JANE TO CASSANDRA,
THURSDAY 4 FEBRUARY 1813

Title page for the first edition of *Pride and Prejudice*, 1813.

PRIDE

AND

PREJUDICE:

A NOVEL.

IN THREE VOLUMES.

———————

BY THE

AUTHOR OF " SENSE AND SENSIBILITY."

———————

VOL. I.

═══════════

ORANGE WINE

The Austens enjoyed all sorts of home-brewed wines and beers, but one of Jane's favourites seems to have been orange wine. On 24 January 1817 she wrote to her friend Alethea Bigg requesting a recipe, while another recipe appears in *Martha Lloyd's Household Book* – a notebook of recipes collected by Jane and Cassandra's friend who lived with them here in Chawton.

   This recipe is perfect for January, when Seville oranges are in season.

To make Orange Wine

Take 2 Gallons of Water let it boil an hour, when it is cold have ready a hundred & twelve pd of Malagoe Raisons picked, & choped small; when the water is quite cold put it on the raisons let it stand a fortnight stirring it twice every day, then strain the liquor from the raison squeeze them very hard, let the liquor run through a hair sive then have ready a Civil Oranges upon pare'd very thin squeeze the juice of the Oranges upon the Peels & put that and the liquor into the Vesel and when it has done working stop it up you may stop it bottle it when fine which will be in about two Months –

I hope you received my little parcel by J. Bond on Wednes
day even[g], my dear Cassandra, & that you will be ready to hear fr
me again on Sunday, for I feel that I must write to you to day.
Your parcel is safely arrived & every thing shall be delivered as it o
Thank you for your note. As you had not heard from me at that
time, it was very good in you to write, but I shall not be so m
your debtor soon. — I want to tell you that I have got my own
darling Child from London; on wednesday I received one Copy, s
down by Falknor, with three lines from Henry to say that he h
given another to Charles & sent a 3[d] by the Coach to Godmersha
just the two Setts which I was least eager for the disposal of.
I wrote to him immediately to beg for my two other setts, unl
he would take the trouble of forwarding them at once to Ste
venton & Portsmouth — not having an idea of his leaving Tow
before to day; — by your account however he was gone before m
Letter was written. The only evil is the delay, nothing mor
can be done till his return. Till James & Mary so, with m
Love. — For your sake I am as well pleased that it sh[d] be
as it might be unpleasant to you to be in the Neighbourho
at the first burst of the business. — The Advertisement is in o
paper to day for the first time; — 18. — He shall ask £1.1.
my two next, & £1.8 for my stupidest of all. — I shall
write to Frank, that he may not think himself neglected.
Miss Benn dined with us on the very day of the Books co
ing & in the even[g] we set fairly at it & read half the

JANE TO CASSANDRA, FRIDAY 29 JANUARY 1813

I hope you received my little parcel by J. Bond on Wednesday eveng, my dear Cassandra, & that you will be ready to hear from me again on Sunday, for I feel that I must write to you to day. Your parcel is safely arrived & everything shall be delivered as it ought. Thank you for your note. As you had not heard from me at that time it was very good in you to write, but I shall not be so much your debtor soon.–I want to tell you that I have got my own darling Child from London;–on Wednesday I received one Copy, sent down by Falknor, with three lines from Henry to say that he had given another to Charles & sent a 3ᵈ by the Coach to Godmersham; just the two Sets which I was least eager for the disposal of. I wrote to him immediately to beg for my two other Sets, unless he would take the trouble of forwarding them at once to Steventon & Portsmouth–not having an idea of his leaving Town before to day;–by your account however he was gone before my Letter was written. The only evil is the delay, nothing more can be done till his return. Tell James & Mary so, with my Love.–For your sake I am as well pleased that it shᵈ be so, as it might be unpleasant to you to be in the Neighbourhood at the first burst of the business.–The Advertisement is in our paper to day for the first time;–18ˢ–He shall ask £1-1- for my two next, & £1-8- for my stupidest of all.–I shall write to Frank, that he may not think himself neglected. Miss Benn dined with us on the very day of the Books coming, & in the eveng we set fairly at it & read half the 1ˢᵗ vol. to her–prefacing that having intelligence from Henry that such a work wᵈ soon appear we had desired him to send it whenever it came out–& I beleive it passed with her unsuspected.–She was amused, poor soul! that she cᵈ not help you know, with two such people to lead the way; but she really does seem to admire Elizabeth. I must confess that I think her as delightful a creature as ever appeared in print, & how I shall be able to tolerate those who do not like her at least, I do not know.

23

Transcript © Deirdre Le Faye, 2011, *Jane Austen's Letters.*

JANE AUSTEN'S MUSIC BOOKS

In the eighteenth century, sheet music was expensive to buy. Instead, it was common for young ladies to borrow or hire their favourite music and then copy it out into books of pre-ruled manuscript paper. Jane Austen's House holds two such books of sheet music, copied out by Jane Austen between 1790 and 1810.

This arrangement of *Nos Galan*, or 'New Year's Eve', is a traditional Welsh winter carol. Today, it is instantly recognizable as the popular Christmas carol *Deck the Halls* – albeit with a few unexpected twists and turns. It is a bright, warming melody that suits cold weather and dark evenings.

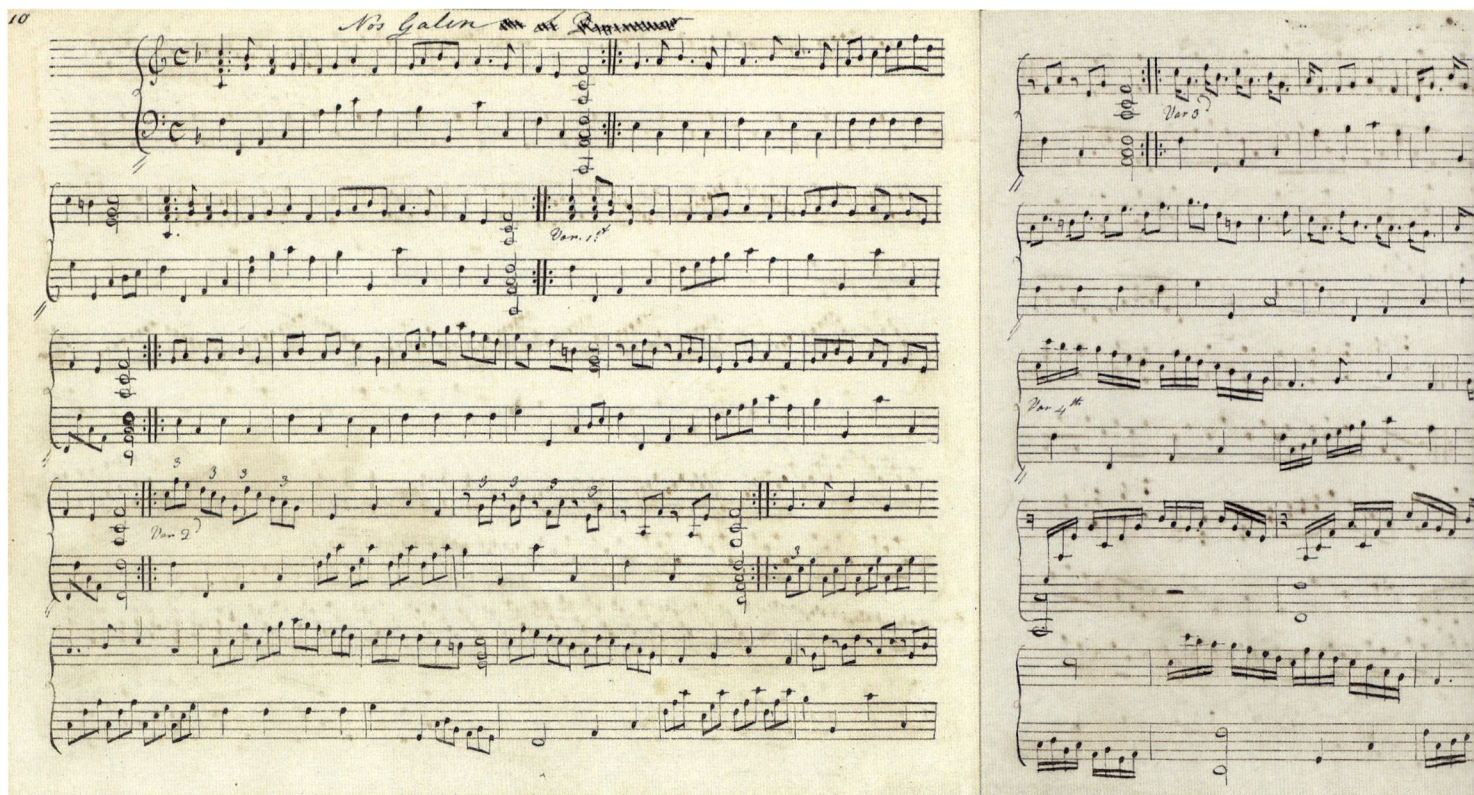

The Clementi
square piano at
Jane Austen's
House dates from
1813, the year
that *Pride and
Prejudice* was first
published.

THE FRENCH REVOLUTION

The French Revolution raged throughout Jane Austen's teenage years, from 1789 until 1799, striking terror into British society and sending France into a state of violent chaos. The French monarchy was overthrown and a Republic put in its place, based on the revolutionary ideals of 'Liberté, Égalité, Fraternité' (Liberty, Equality, Fraternity).

In 1791 a new constitution was completed, giving power to an elected assembly. In June, the French King Louis XVI tried to escape France, but was caught and returned to Paris. He was brought to trial for treason and executed by guillotine on 21 January 1793. His wife, the infamous Marie Antoinette, was executed nine months later.

The Revolution continued to rage, with Robespierre and the Committee of Public Safety taking over political power. Between 1793 and 1794, the Reign of Terror saw 16,000 'counter-revolutionaries' executed in a bloodbath that shocked the world.

For the Austens, the French Revolution was closer to home than one might think. Jane's cousin Eliza was married to the Comte de Feuillide, a captain in Marie Antoinette's Regiment of Dragoons and an ardent Royalist.

In September 1792, at the height of the Terror, Eliza was staying with the Austens at Steventon.

Copperplate engraving of the execution of Louis XVI, by Georg Heinrich Sieveking.

She wrote to her cousin Phila Walter:

'I can readily believe that the share of sensibility I know you to be possessed of would not suffer you to learn the tragical events of which France has of late been the theatre, without being much affected. My private letters confirm the intelligence afforded by Public prints, and assure me that nothing we read there is exaggerated. M. de F. is at present in Paris. He had determined on coming to England, but finds it impossible to get away.'

The Comte made several visits to England, but in February 1794 he fell foul of the Revolution and was executed at the guillotine. It is possible that Eliza was staying in Steventon when she heard of her husband's death, bringing the Revolution dramatically and tragically into the Hampshire countryside.

FEBRUARY

RIGHT
Watercolour
portrait of Jane
and Cassandra's
niece Fanny
Knight, by
Cassandra Austen.

31

'You are inimitable, irresistible.
You are the delight of my Life.
Such Letters, such entertaining
Letters, as you have lately sent!–
Such a description of your queer
little heart!–Such a lovely display
of what Imagination does.–You
are worth your weight in Gold, or
even in the new Silver Coinage.'

JANE TO FANNY KNIGHT,
TUESDAY 20 FEBRUARY 1817

Captain Wentworth's letter to *Anne Elliot* in Persuasion *is often described as the most romantic letter in English literature. The scene takes place on a rainy day in February at The White Hart in Bath, a busy coaching inn that Jane knew and referred to in a letter of her own in 1813.*

CAPTAIN WENTWORTH'S LETTER

She had only time, however, to move closer to the table where he had been writing, when footsteps were heard returning; the door opened, it was himself. He begged their pardon, but he had forgotten his gloves, and instantly crossing the room to the writing table, he drew out a letter from under the scattered paper, placed it before Anne with eyes of glowing entreaty fixed on her for a time, and hastily collecting his gloves, was again out of the room, almost before Mrs Musgrove was aware of his being in it: the work of an instant!

The revolution which one instant had made in Anne, was almost beyond expression. The letter, with a direction hardly legible, to 'Miss A. E.--,' was evidently the one which he had been folding so hastily. While supposed to be writing only to Captain Benwick, he had been also addressing her! On the contents of that letter depended all which this world could do for her. Anything was possible, anything might be defied rather than suspense. Mrs Musgrove had little arrangements of her own at her own table; to their protection she must trust, and sinking into the chair which he had occupied, succeeding to the very spot where he had leaned and written, her eyes devoured the following words:

'I can listen no longer in silence. I must speak to you by such means as are within my reach. You pierce my soul. I am half agony, half hope. Tell me not that I am too late, that such precious feelings are gone for ever. I offer myself to you again with a heart even more your own than when you almost broke it, eight years and a half ago. Dare not say that man forgets sooner than woman, that his love has an earlier death. I have loved none but you. Unjust I may have been, weak and resentful I have been, but never inconstant. You alone have brought me to Bath. For you alone, I think and plan. Have you not seen this? Can you fail to have understood my wishes? I had not waited even these ten days, could I

have read your feelings, as I think you must have penetrated mine. I can hardly write. I am every instant hearing something which overpowers me. You sink your voice, but I can distinguish the tones of that voice when they would be lost on others. Too good, too excellent creature! You do us justice, indeed. You do believe that there is true attachment and constancy among men. Believe it to be most fervent, most undeviating, in F. W.

'I must go, uncertain of my fate; but I shall return hither, or follow your party, as soon as possible. A word, a look, will be enough to decide whether I enter your father's house this evening or never.'

Such a letter was not to be soon recovered from. Half an hour's solitude and reflection might have tranquillized her; but the ten minutes only which now passed before she was interrupted, with all the restraints of her situation, could do nothing towards tranquillity. Every moment rather brought fresh agitation. It was overpowering happiness. And before she was beyond the first stage of full sensation, Charles, Mary, and Henrietta all came in.

The absolute necessity of seeming like herself produced then an immediate struggle; but after a while she could do no more. She began not to understand a word they said, and was obliged to plead indisposition and excuse herself. They could then see that she looked very ill, were shocked and concerned, and would not stir without her for the world. This was dreadful. Would they only have gone away, and left her in the quiet possession of that room it would have been her cure; but to have them all standing or waiting around her was distracting, and in desperation, she said she would go home.

PERSUASION, VOLUME II, CHAPTER 11

PHILADELPHIA HANCOCK

Philadelphia was Jane Austen's aunt on her father's side. She was a glamorous figure, with more than a hint of mystery and scandal about her. A beautiful girl, she was orphaned at a young age and apprenticed to a milliner in Covent Garden. At the age of 21, she found her way onto a ship bound for India and sailed for Madras. Her intention was certainly to find a husband, which she promptly did, marrying Mr Tysoe Saul Hancock, a surgeon employed by the East India Company, in February 1753.

In 1761, Philadelphia had a daughter, Elizabeth, later known as Eliza – Jane Austen's adored older cousin. Eliza's godfather was Warren Hastings, the first Governor of India, and it was rumoured that he was really her father. He was certainly very fond of her, giving her lavish presents; in 1772 he gave her £5,000 and three years later he gave a further £5,000. The money went into a trust for Eliza which generated an income of about £400 a year – around £50,000 in today's money.

In 1765, Philadelphia returned to England where Eliza could have access to the best tutors, and where she could enjoy fashionable London society. This lovely miniature portrait of her is thought to have been painted shortly after they returned to England by the leading miniaturist of the day, John Smart. Originally Mr Hancock wore it in a ring. He bequeathed it to Eliza with the wish that she would never part with it, and she is thought to have had it converted into a brooch.

After her husband's death in 1775, Philadelphia took Eliza to live on the continent where their fashionable style of living could be achieved with less expense. She died on 26 February 1792.

Miniature of Philadelphia Hancock by John Smart, c.1770.

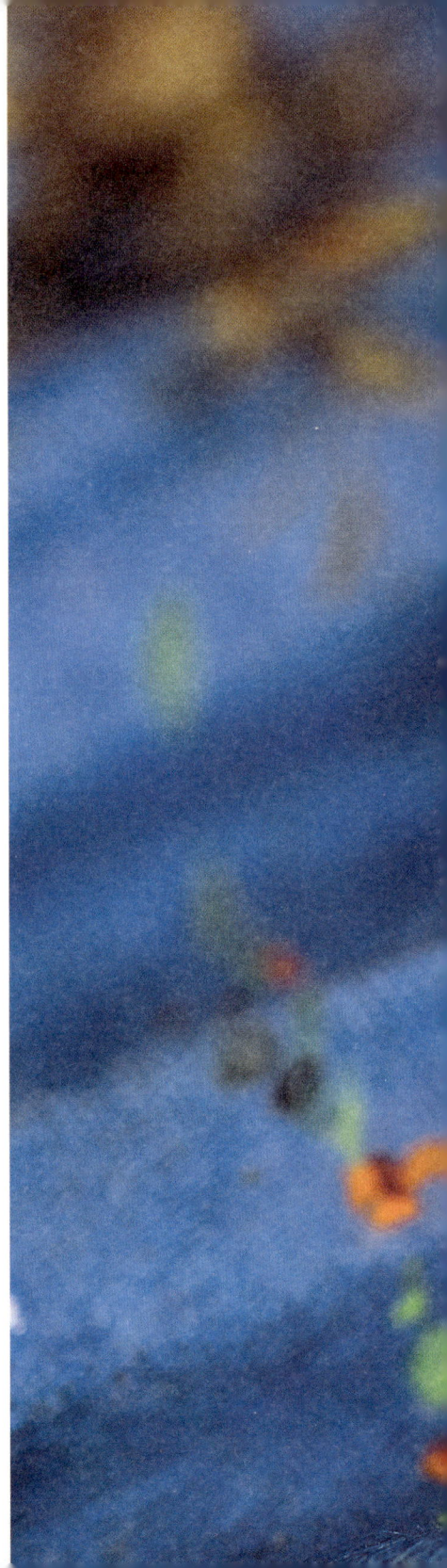

to you all for your praise; it came at a right time, for I had
some fits of disgust;—our 2d evening's reading to Miss Benn had not pleased
me so well, but I beleive something must be attributed to my Mother's
too rapid way of getting on—& tho' she perfectly understands the Charac-
ters herself, she cannot speak as they ought.—Upon the whole however
I am quite vain enough & well satisfied enough.—The work is rather
too light & bright & sparkling;—it wants shade;—it wants to be stretched
out here & there with a long Chapter—of sense if it could be had, if not
of solemn specious nonsense—about something unconnected with the story;
an Essay on Writing, a critique on Walter Scott, or the history of Buona-
parte—or anything that would form a contrast & bring the reader with
increased delight to the playfulness & Epigrammatism of the general
stile.—I doubt your quite agreeing with me here—I know your too par-
tial admirer to feel as you ought about it.—The caution observed at Steventon with regard to the possession
of the Books is an agreable surprise to me, & I heartily wish it may
be the means of saving you from everything unpleasant;—but you
must be prepared for the Neighbourhood being perhaps already in-
formed of there being such a work in the World, & in the Chawton
World!—Dummer will do that you know.—It was spoken of
here one morning when Mrs D. called with Miss Benn.—The greatest blun-
der in the Printing that I have met with is in Page 220—Vol. 3.
where two speeches are made into one.—There might as well
have been no suppers at Longbourn, but I suppose it was the
remains of Mrs Bennet's old Meryton habits.—I am sorry for
your disappointment about Manydown, & fear this week must
be a dead loss to you.—As Ladies one may venture to judge at a dista

JANE TO CASSANDRA, THURSDAY 4 FEBRUARY 1813

My dear Cassandra

Your letter was truely welcome & I am much obliged to you all for your praise; it came at a right time, for I had had some fits of disgust;—our 2ᵈ evening's reading to Miss Benn had not pleased me so well, but I beleive something must be attributed to my Mother's too rapid way of getting on—& tho' she perfectly understands the Characters herself, she cannot speak as they ought.—Upon the whole however I am quite vain enough & well satisfied enough.—The work is rather too light & bright & sparkling;—it wants shade;—it wants to be stretched out here & there with a long Chapter—of sense if it could be had, if not of solemn specious nonsense— about something unconnected with the story; an Essay on Writing, a critique on Walter Scott, or the history of Buonaparté—or anything that would form a contrast & bring the reader with increased delight to the playfulness & Epigrammatism of the general stile.—I doubt your quite agreeing with me here.—I know your starched Notions—The caution observed at Steventon with regard to the possession of the Book is an agreable surprise to me, & I heartily wish it may be the means of saving you from everything unpleasant;—but you must be prepared for the Neighbourhood being perhaps already informed of there being such a Work in the World, & in the Chawton World! Drummer will do <u>that</u> you know.—It was spoken of here one mornᵍ when Mʳˢ D. called with Miss Benn.—The greatest blunder in the Printing that I have met with is in Page 220—Vol. 3. where two speeches are made into one.—There might as well have been no suppers at Longbourn, but I suppose it was the remains of Mʳˢ Bennet's old Meryton habits.—I am sorry for your disappointment about Manydown, & fear this week must be a heavy one. As far as one may venture to judge at a distance of 20 miles you must miss Martha. For <u>her</u> sake I was glad to hear of her going, as I suppose she must have been growing anxious, & wanting to be again in scenes of agitation & exertion.—She had a lovely day for her journey. I walked to Alton, & dirt excepted, found it delightful,—it seemed like an old Febʸ. come back again.—

Transcript © Deirdre Le Faye, 2011, *Jane Austen's Letters*.

SALVES AND OINTMENTS

Herbal treatments were commonly used in the Austens' time to cure most of the day-to-day ailments that occurred within the family. Most country people grew their own medicinal plants that could be picked and made into a medicine or tisane when needed.

The Austen women kept their own bees, so they would have had beeswax readily available to make this simple ointment to soothe chapped winter lips. It is coloured with alkanet root – a herbaceous plant in the borage family whose roots were used to produce a red dye.

This recipe is from *Martha Lloyd's Household Book* and may well have been mixed up in the kitchen at Chawton. The recipe is attributed to Mrs Fowle, a family friend and the mother of Tom Fowle, to whom Cassandra was engaged.

A good salve for sore Lips

Take an oz: of Bee's-wax; put it into an oz: of good Salad Oyl, melt it over the fire & colour it with alkany root; when it has boil'd & is of a fine red, strain it and drop in three penny-worth of Balsam of peru, then pour it into the bottom of tea Cups that it may turn out in cakes. –

Mrs. Fowle

STAGE PRODUCTION OF *PRIDE AND PREJUDICE* AT ST JAMES THEATRE, LONDON

The first big-budget theatrical version of *Pride and Prejudice* was Helen Jerome's sparky adaptation, which enjoyed a successful run on Broadway in 1935. The following year it transferred to London's West End, opening on 27 February 1936 at the St James Theatre with a new British cast. Elizabeth Bennet was played by Celia Johnson, a rising star who later made her name in the film *Brief Encounter*.

The UK production also featured new sets and costumes designed by Rex Whistler, one of the most dazzling and diverse artists of the interwar period. His costume designs for *Pride and Prejudice* show his light touch, elegance and sense of humour.

The production was highly influential, putting more focus on Mr Darcy than the original novel and turning him into the sexy heartthrob we know today. It also subdued Austen's exploration of

female independence, turning Lizzy into a weepy heroine who frequently trembled and cried, and who declared to Darcy after his second proposal 'I am abased'.

Although Jerome's version of a weakened Elizabeth has not survived in contemporary depictions of the character, her portrayal of a sexy Darcy as a second central character persists to this day.

Costume designs for *Pride and Prejudice*, by Rex Whistler. From left to right: Mrs Bennet, Lady Catherine de Bourgh, Lady Catherine de Bourgh, Elizabeth Bennet, Mrs Gardiner, Lydia Bennet.

'Mrs Day has now got the Carpet in hand, & Monday I hope will be the last day of her employment here. A fortnight afterwards she is to be called again from the shades of her red-check'd bed in an alley near the end of the High Street to clean the new House & air the Bedding.'

JANE TO CASSANDRA,
SATURDAY 21 FEBRUARY 1807

42

SPRING CLEANING

Conservation cleaning takes place at Jane Austen's House throughout the year, but the cold spring months, when the House is not open every day of the week, provide the opportunity to do a deep clean. Volunteers help with the dusting and polishing, furniture is moved, windows are cleaned and light spills into dark corners.

MARCH

'A cold day, but bright & clean.—I am afraid your planting can hardly have begun.—I am sorry to hear that there has been a rise in tea. I do not mean to pay Twining till later in the day, when we may order a fresh supply.'

JANE TO CASSANDRA,
SUNDAY 6 MARCH 1814

CASSANDRA AUSTEN

Cassandra was three years older than her sister Jane and the two were best friends all their lives. Cassandra was pretty, practical and sensible and, although she is often pictured as the more solemn of the two sisters, Jane at least thought she was extremely funny. In a letter from 1796 she wrote:

**'My dearest Cassandra
The letter which I have this
moment received from you has
diverted me beyond moderation.
I could die of laughter at it,
as they used to say at school.
You are indeed the finest comic
writer of the present age.'**

At around the age of 19, Cassandra became engaged to Tom Fowle, but he died tragically on a trip to the Caribbean and she never married. Instead, she took on the role of homemaker, sister-in-law and aunt, staying for long periods at Godmersham to help with their brother Edward's large family.

Here at the house in Chawton, Cassandra took on most of the household management, leaving her mother to tend the garden, Martha to help with the cooking and Jane to write.

Cassandra was a keen amateur artist. As a teenager she illustrated Jane's mock history book, *A History of England*, creating characters that are funny and beautiful, if not accurate. We are also indebted to her for the two authenticated likenesses of Jane that we know today: a back view of her in a blue dress and an unfinished sketch of her face.

After Jane's death in 1817, Cassandra continued living in Chawton for the rest of her life. She kept herself busy, teaching reading and sewing to the village girls, tending the garden and looking after her bees. She had a dog called Link who, it is said, would accompany a manservant to the farm at the end of the road to fetch milk; on the way back, Link would carry the pail of milk in his mouth.

Cassandra died on 22 March 1845 at the age of 72, and was buried in the churchyard of St Nicholas in Chawton, beside her mother.

PLANTING
POTATOES

Many women in the eighteenth century
worked in their gardens, but there are very
few paintings of them doing so. This one
shows a French noblewoman pretending to
be rustic at Versailles.

*The Duchess of
Chaulnes as a
Gardener in an
Allée* by Louis
Carrogis de
Carmontelle, 1771.

Jane's mother, Mrs Austen, did rather more than just play at gardening. At Steventon Rectory, she helped her husband to run a farm of some 200 acres and when the Austen women moved to Chawton, Mrs Austen, at nearly 70 years of age, took on the management of the large garden.

Her great-granddaughter Fanny Caroline Lefroy recorded in her *Family History* manuscript that Mrs Austen:

'found plenty of occupation for herself in gardening and needlework. The former was, with her, no idle pastime, no mere cutting of roses and tying up of flowers. She dug up her own potatoes, and I have no doubt she planted them, for the kitchen garden was as much her delight as the flower borders, and I have heard my mother say that when at work, she wore a green round frock like a day-labourer's.'

Potatoes are normally planted in March, two to four weeks before the last frost.

'The day was uncommonly lovely. It was really March; but it was April in its mild air, brisk soft wind, and bright sun, occasionally clouded for a minute; and everything looked so beautiful under the influence of such a sky, the effects of the shadows pursuing each other on the ships at Spithead and the island beyond, with the ever-varying hues of the sea, now at high water, dancing in its glee and dashing against the ramparts with so fine a sound, produced altogether such a combination of charms for Fanny, as made her gradually almost careless of the circumstances under which she felt them.'

MANSFIELD PARK,
VOLUME III, CHAPTER 11

An illustration of the High Street, Southampton. Image from *Our Own Country*, published 1898.

SOUTHAMPTON

The Austen women moved to Southampton in October 1806 and set about looking for a house. The one they settled on was 'a commodious old-fashioned house' on Castle Square, which they moved into in March 1807.

It was a busy household consisting of Jane, Cassandra and Mrs Austen as well as Frank and his new wife Mary Gibson, who was heavily pregnant. The plan was for the Austen women to support Mary while Frank was away at sea, while he contributed to the household finances. They were also joined by their old friend Martha Lloyd, after the death of her own mother the previous year left her without a home.

Jane described the house in Castle Square to Cassandra, who was away at Godmersham while it was being fixed up. In February, she wrote: 'We hear that we are envied our House by many people, & that the Garden is the best in the Town.'

In another letter she described the garden with a delight that makes one realize how much she had missed the countryside during their years in Bath:

'Our Garden is putting in order, by a Man who bears a remarkably good Character, has a very fine complexion & asks something less than the first. The Shrubs which border the gravel walk he says are only sweetbriar & roses, & the latter of an indifferent sort;—we mean to get a few of a better kind therefore, & at my own particular desire he procures us some Syringas. I could not do without a Syringa, for the sake of Cowper's Line.—We talk also of a Laburnam.— The Border under the Terrace Wall, is clearing away to receive Currants & Gooseberry Bushes, & a spot is found very proper for Raspberries.'

JANE TO CASSANDRA, SUNDAY 8 FEBRUARY 1807

JANE AUSTEN 'SCRAPS'

Shortly before her death in 1845 Cassandra destroyed many of Jane's surviving letters, an act that was much criticized by later generations of critics, although today it is believed that she acted to protect Jane's memory and reputation. Considering Jane's sharp tongue, it may have also been to protect her family from her hurtful comments.

Cassandra distributed the remaining letters among the family and to admirers of her sister's writings, kickstarting a mania for Jane Austen 'scraps' that continues to this day.

This fragment of writing in Jane Austen's hand is known as the 'Sermon Scrap'; it is part of a sermon written by James Austen in 1814, copied out by Jane. It was discovered glued into the front of a copy of James Edward Austen-Leigh's *A Memoir of Jane Austen* (1870) along with a note stating: 'this is the hand writing, not the composition, of my Aunt Jane Austen, Authoress of *Pride & Prejudice*.'

The scrap echoes a discussion in *Mansfield Park* on the 'art of reading' and its importance to the modern clergyman. It reads:

'Men may get into a habit of repeating the words of our Prayers by rote, perhaps without thoroughly understanding, — certainly without thoroughly feeling their full force & meaning.'

ROSINGS PARK

In Pride and Prejudice, *Lizzy's trip to Hunsford takes place in March. This episode introduces Mr Collins's humble abode, the grandeur of Rosings Park and the attentive neighbourliness of Lady Catherine de Bourgh.*

At length the Parsonage was discernible. The garden sloping to the road, the house standing in it, the green pales, and the laurel hedge, everything declared they were arriving. Mr. Collins and Charlotte appeared at the door, and the carriage stopped at the small gate which led by a short gravel walk to the house, amidst the nods and smiles of the whole party. In a moment they were all out of the chaise, rejoicing at the sight of each other. Mrs. Collins welcomed her friend with the liveliest pleasure, and Elizabeth was more and more satisfied with coming when she found herself so affectionately received. She saw instantly that her cousin's manners were not altered by his marriage; his formal civility was just what it had been, and he

Illustration by Joan Hassall for *Pride and Prejudice* (Folio Society, 1957).

detained her some minutes at the gate to hear and satisfy his enquiries after all her family. They were then, with no other delay than his pointing out the neatness of the entrance, taken into the house; and as soon as they were in the parlour, he welcomed them a second time, with ostentatious formality to his humble abode, and punctually repeated all his wife's offers of refreshment.

Elizabeth was prepared to see him in his glory; and she could not help in fancying that in displaying the good proportion of the room, its aspect and its furniture, he addressed himself particularly to her, as if wishing to make her feel what she had lost in refusing him. But though everything seemed neat and comfortable, she was not able to gratify him by any sigh of repentance, and rather looked with wonder at her friend that she could have so cheerful an air with such a companion. When Mr. Collins said anything of which his wife might reasonably be ashamed, which certainly was not unseldom, she involuntarily turned her eye on Charlotte. Once or twice she could discern a faint blush; but in general Charlotte wisely did not hear. After sitting long enough to admire every article of furniture in the room, from the sideboard to the fender, to give an account of their journey, and of all that had happened in London, Mr. Collins invited them to take a stroll in the garden, which was large and well laid out, and to the cultivation of which he attended himself. To work in this garden was one of his most respectable pleasures; and Elizabeth admired the command of countenance with which Charlotte talked of the healthfulness of the exercise, and owned she encouraged it as much as possible. Here, leading the way through every walk and cross walk, and scarcely allowing them an interval to utter the praises he asked for, every view was pointed out with a minuteness which left beauty entirely behind. He could number the fields in every direction, and could tell how many trees there were in the most distant clump. But of all the views which his garden, or which the country or kingdom could boast, none were to be compared with the prospect of Rosings, afforded by an opening in the trees that bordered the park nearly opposite the front of his house. It was a handsome modern building, well situated on rising ground.

From his garden, Mr. Collins would have led them round his two meadows; but the ladies, not having shoes to encounter the remains of a white frost, turned back; and while Sir William accompanied him, Charlotte took her sister and friend over the house, extremely well pleased, probably, to have the opportunity of showing it without her husband's help. It was rather small, but well built and convenient; and everything was fitted up and arranged with a neatness and consistency of which Elizabeth gave Charlotte all the credit. When Mr. Collins could be forgotten, there was really an air of great comfort throughout, and by Charlotte's evident enjoyment of it, Elizabeth supposed he must be often forgotten.

PRIDE AND PREJUDICE, VOLUME II, CHAPTER 5

JANE TO CAROLINE AUSTEN, WEDNESDAY 13 MARCH 1816

Chawton Wednesday
March 13.

My dear Caroline

I am very glad to have an opportunity of answering your agreable little Letter. You seem to be quite my own Neice in your feelings towards M^{de} de Genlis. I do not think I could even now, at my sedate time of Life, read Olimpe et Theophile without being in a Rage. It really is too bad!–Not allowing them to be happy together, when they are married.–Don't talk of it, pray. I have just lent your Aunt Frank the 1st vol. of Les Veilles du Chateau, for Mary Jane to read. It will be some time before she comes to the horror of Olympe.–We have had sad weather lately, I hope you have liked it.–Our Pond is brimful & our roads are dirty & our walls are damp, & we sit wishing every bad day may be the last. It is not cold however. Another week perhaps may see us shrinking & shivering under a dry East Wind.

I had a very nice Letter from your Brother not long ago, & I am quite happy to see how much his Hand is improving.–I am convinced that it will end in a very gentlemanlike Hand, much above Par.–We have had a great deal of fun lately with Post-chaises stopping at the door; three times within a few days, we had a couple of agreable Visitors turn in unexpectedly–your Uncle Henry & Mr Tilson, Mrs Heathcote & Miss Bigg, your Uncle Henry & Mr Seymour. Take notice, that it was the same Uncle Henry each time.

I remain my dear Caroline
Your affec: Aunt
J. Austen

Miss C. Austen
Steventon

Transcript © Deirdre Le Faye, 2011, Jane Austen's Letters.

I had a very nice Letter from your
Brother not long ago, & I am quite
happy to see how much his Hand
is improving. — I am convinced that
it will end in a very gentleman
like Hand, much above Par. —
We have had a great deal of fun
lately with Post chaises stopping
at the door; three times within
a few days we had a couple of
agreeable Visitors turn in unexpect=
=edly. — Your Uncle & Mr. Tilson,
Mrs. Heathcote & Miss Biggs,

APRIL

This watercolour drawing of a landscape was painted by Anna Lefroy, Jane Austen's niece.

Anna was the daughter of Jane's eldest brother, James. She grew up at Steventon Rectory, just as Jane did, and made several sketches and watercolours of the surrounding area.

While this watercolour drawing is undated, it is easy to imagine that it shows Hampshire in the springtime, with a brisk April breeze stirring the new leaves on the trees.

'The morning was fine and dry, and Marianne, in her plan of employment abroad, had not calculated for any change of weather during their stay at Cleveland. With great surprise therefore, did she find herself prevented by a settled rain from going out again after dinner. She had depended on a twilight walk to the Grecian temple, and perhaps all over the grounds, and an evening merely cold or damp would not have deterred her from it; but a heavy and settled rain even she could not fancy dry or pleasant weather for walking.'

SENSE AND SENSIBILITY,
VOLUME III, CHAPTER 6

REVEREND AND MRS AUSTEN

Jane's father George Austen was born in Tonbridge, Kent in 1731; as a child he was orphaned and sent to live with relatives. He attended St John's College, Oxford, where he was awarded a Fellowship, and in 1755 he was ordained at Rochester Cathedral. He was a scholarly and gentle man. Tall, slim and good-looking with chestnut brown hair and bright hazel eyes, he was known as 'the handsome Proctor' during his time at Oxford.

At some point in the early 1760s George Austen met Cassandra Leigh, a handsome and clever young woman with aristocratic connections and plenty of sparkle and spirit. They became engaged and were married on 26 April 1764 at St Swithin's Church in Walcot, Bath. The service was taken by Cassandra's friend Tom Lybbe-Powys, with her brother and sister acting as witnesses; her wedding dress was a practical and striking red riding habit. The couple set off for Hampshire immediately after the service, spending the night in Andover on their way to the village of Deane, where they began their married life.

The Austens set up home in Deane Rectory, just over a mile from Steventon where George was Rector, and moved to Steventon Rectory, Jane's childhood home, in 1768. In all they had eight children, of whom Jane, their second daughter, was the second to youngest.

It was a busy household. Alongside George's church duties, the Austens ran a small school at home, taking in boy pupils as boarders, as well as managing a 200-acre farm.

St Nicholas Church, Steventon.

DARCY'S PROPOSAL

Darcy's first proposal to Elizabeth takes place in April, while she is staying at Hunsford Parsonage. We know this because later in the novel, when he proposes for a second time, he says 'If your feelings are still what they were last April, tell me so at once.'

Illustration by Joan Hassall for *Pride and Prejudice* (Folio Society, 1957).

While settling this point, she was suddenly roused by the sound of the door-bell, and her spirits were a little fluttered by the idea of its being Colonel Fitzwilliam himself, who had once before called late in the evening, and might now come to enquire particularly after her. But this idea was soon banished, and her spirits were very differently affected, when, to her utter amazement, she saw Mr. Darcy walk into the room. In an hurried manner he immediately began an enquiry after her health, imputing his visit to a wish of hearing that she were better. She answered him with cold civility. He sat down for a few moments, and then getting up, walked about the room. Elizabeth was surprised, but said not a word. After a silence of several minutes, he came towards her in an agitated manner, and thus began:

'In vain I have struggled. It will not do. My feelings will not be repressed. You must allow me to tell you how ardently I admire and love you.'

Elizabeth's astonishment was beyond expression. She stared, coloured, doubted, and was silent. This he considered sufficient encouragement; and the avowal of all that he felt, and had long felt for her, immediately followed. He spoke well; but there were feelings besides those of the heart to be detailed; and he was not more eloquent on the subject of tenderness than of pride. His sense of her inferiority—of its being a degradation—of the family obstacles which had always opposed to inclination, were dwelt on with a warmth which seemed due to the consequence he was wounding, but was very unlikely to recommend his suit.

In spite of her deeply-rooted dislike, she could not be insensible to the compliment of such a man's affection, and though her intentions did not vary for an instant, she was at first sorry for the pain he was to receive; till, roused to resentment by his subsequent language, she lost all compassion in anger. She tried, however, to compose herself to answer him with patience, when he should have done. He concluded with representing to her the strength of that attachment which, in spite of all his endeavours, he had found impossible to conquer; and with expressing his hope that it would now be rewarded by her acceptance of his hand. As he said this, she could easily see that he had no doubt of a favourable answer. He spoke of apprehension and anxiety, but his countenance expressed real security. Such a circumstance could only exasperate farther, and, when he ceased, the colour rose into her cheeks, and she said:

'In such cases as this, it is, I believe, the established mode to express a sense of obligation for the sentiments avowed, however unequally they may be returned. It is natural that obligation should be felt, and if I could *feel* gratitude, I would now thank you. But I cannot—I have never desired your good opinion, and you have certainly bestowed it most unwillingly. I am sorry to have occasioned pain to anyone. It has been most unconsciously done, however, and I hope will be of short duration. The feelings which, you tell me, have long prevented the acknowledgment of your regard, can have little difficulty in overcoming it after this explanation.'

Mr. Darcy, who was leaning against the mantelpiece with his eyes fixed on her face, seemed to catch her words with no less resentment than surprise. His complexion became pale with anger, and the disturbance of his mind was visible in every feature. He was struggling for the appearance of composure, and would not open his lips till he believed himself to have attained it. The pause was to Elizabeth's feelings dreadful. At length, with a voice of forced calmness, he said:

'And this is all the reply which I am to have the honour of expecting! I might, perhaps, wish to be informed why, with so little *endeavour* at civility, I am thus rejected. But it is of small importance.'

'I might as well enquire,' replied she, 'why with so evident a desire of offending and insulting me, you chose to tell me that you liked me against your will, against your reason, and even against your character? Was not this some excuse for incivility, if I *was* uncivil? But I have other provocations. You know I have. Had not my feelings decided against you—had they been indifferent, or had they even been favourable, do you think that any consideration would tempt me to accept the man who has been the means of ruining, perhaps for ever, the happiness of a most beloved sister?'

As she pronounced these words, Mr. Darcy changed colour; but the emotion was short, and he listened without attempting to interrupt her while she continued:

'I have every reason in the world to think ill of you. No motive can excuse the unjust and ungenerous part you acted *there*. You dare not, you cannot deny, that you have been the principal, if not the only means of dividing them from each other—of exposing one to the censure of the world for caprice and instability, and the other to its derision for disappointed hopes, and involving them both in misery of the acutest kind.'

She paused, and saw with no slight indignation that he was listening with an air which proved him wholly unmoved by any feeling of remorse. He even looked at her with a smile of affected incredulity.

'Can you deny that you have done it?' she repeated.

With assumed tranquillity he then replied: 'I have no wish of denying that I did everything in my power to separate my friend from your sister, or that I rejoice in my success. Towards *him* I have been kinder than towards myself.'

PRIDE AND PREJUDICE, VOLUME II, CHAPTER 11

JANE TO REVEREND JAMES STANIER CLARKE, MONDAY 1 APRIL 1816

My dear Sir

I am honoured by the Prince's thanks, & very much obliged to yourself for the kind manner on which You mention the Work. I have also to acknowledge a former Letter, forwarded to me from Hans Place. I assure You I felt very grateful for the friendly Tenor of it, & hope my silence will have been considered as it was truly meant, to proceed only from an unwillingness to tax your Time with idle Thanks.—

Under every interesting circumstance which your own Talents & literary Labours have placed you in, or the favour of the Regent bestowed, you have my best wishes. Your recent appointments I hope are a step to something still better. In my opinion, The service of a Court can hardly be too well paid, for immense must be the sacrifice of Time & Feeling required by it.

You are very, very kind in your hints as to the sort of Composition which might recommend me at present, & I am fully sensible that an Historical Romance, founded on the House of Saxe Cobourg might be much more to the purpose of Profit or Popularity, than such pictures of domestic Life in Country Villages as I deal in—but I could no more write a Romance than an Epic Poem.— I could not sit seriously down to write a serious Romance under any other motive than to save my Life, & if it were indispensable for me to keep it up & never relax into laughing at myself or other people, I am sure I should be hung before I had finished the first Chapter. —No— I must keep to my own style & go on in my own Way; And though I may never succeed again in that, I am convinced that I should totally fail in any other.—

I remain my dear Sir,
Your very much obliged & very sincere friend
J. Austen

Chawton near Alton April lst–
1816–

My dear Sir

I am honoured by the Prince's thanks, &
very much obliged to yourself for the kind manner
which you mention the Work. I have also to
knowledge a former Letter, forwarded to me from Hans
Place. I assure you I felt very grateful for the friendly
tenor of it, & hope my silence will have been considered
it was truely meant, to proceed only from an uncivil-
ingness to tax your Time with idle Thanks.
Under every interesting circumstance which your own Talent
& literary Labours have placed you in, or the Favour of
the Regent bestowed, you have my best wishes. Your
recent appointments I hope are a step to something better still.
In my opinion, the service of a Court can hardly be
too well paid, for immense must be the sacrifice
of Time & Feeling they must make who live
immersed.

You are very, very kind in your hints as to
the sort of Composition which might recommend me
at present, & I am fully sensible that an Historical

'Ever since the day—about four years ago—that Miss Taylor and I met with him in Broadway Lane, when, because it began to drizzle, he darted away with so much gallantry, and borrowed two umbrellas for us from Farmer Mitchell's, I made up my mind on the subject. I planned the match from that hour; and when such success has blessed me in this instance, dear papa, you cannot think that I shall leave off match-making.'

EMMA, VOLUME I, CHAPTER 1

St Nicholas
Church, Chawton.

71

BAKED APPLES

*In the winter and spring, fruit and vegetables were
carefully stored, cooked and preserved to make
them last. In Chawton, the Austen women were
lucky enough to have an orchard, unlike Miss Bates
in* Emma *who, living in town, had no garden of her
own and was reliant on Mr Knightley's largesse...*

'"Oh!" said he, "I can fasten the rivet. I like a job of that sort excessively." I never shall forget his manner. And when I brought out the baked apples from the closet, and hoped our friends would be so very obliging as to take some, "Oh!" said he directly, "there is nothing in the way of fruit half so good, and these are the finest-looking home-baked apples I ever saw in my life." That, you know, was so very.... And I am sure, by his manner, it was no compliment. Indeed they are very delightful apples, and Mrs. Wallis does them full justice—only we do not have them baked more than twice, and Mr. Woodhouse made us promise to have them done three times—but Miss Woodhouse will be so good as not to mention it. The apples themselves are the very finest sort for baking, beyond a doubt; all from Donwell—some of Mr. Knightley's most liberal supply. He sends us a sack every year; and certainly there never was such a keeping apple anywhere as one of his trees—I believe there is two of them. My mother says the orchard was always famous in her younger days. But I was really quite shocked the other day—for Mr. Knightley called one morning, and Jane was eating these apples, and we talked about them and said how much she enjoyed them, and he asked whether we were not got to the end of our stock. "I am sure you must be," said he, "and I will send you another supply; for I have a great many more than I can ever use. William Larkins let me keep a larger quantity than usual this year. I will send you some more, before they get good for nothing." So I begged he would not—for really as to ours being gone, I could not absolutely say that we had a great many left—it was but half a dozen indeed; but they should be all kept for Jane; and I could not at all bear that he should be sending us more, so liberal as he had been already; and Jane said the same. And when he was gone, she almost quarrelled with me—No, I should not say quarrelled, for we never had a quarrel in our lives; but she was quite distressed that I had owned the apples were so nearly gone; she wished I had made him believe we had a great many left. Oh, said I, my dear, I did say as much as I could. However, the very same evening William Larkins came over with a large basket of apples, the same sort of apples, a bushel at least, and I was very much obliged, and went down and spoke to William Larkins and said every thing, as you may suppose. William Larkins is such an old acquaintance! I am always glad to see him. But, however, I found afterwards from Patty, that William said it was all the apples of that sort his master had; he had brought them all—and now his master had not one left to bake or boil. William did not seem to mind it himself, he was so pleased to think his master had sold so many; for William, you know, thinks more of his master's profit than any thing; but Mrs. Hodges, he said, was quite displeased at their being all sent away. She could not bear that her master should not be able to have another apple-tart this spring.'

EMMA, VOLUME II, CHAPTER 9

'She had not known before what pleasures she had to lose in passing March and April in a town. She had not known before how much the beginnings and progress of vegetation had delighted her. What animation, both of body and mind, she had derived from watching the advance of that season which cannot, in spite of its capriciousness, be unlovely, and seeing its increasing beauties from the earliest flowers in the warmest divisions of her aunt's garden, to the opening of leaves of her uncle's plantations, and the glory of his woods.'

MANSFIELD PARK,
VOLUME III, CHAPTER 14

MAY

'How lucky we were in our weather yesterday!—This wet morning makes one more sensible of it. We had no rain of any consequence; the head of the Curricle was put half-up three or four times, but our share of the Showers was very trifling, though they seemed to be heavy all round us, when we were on the Hog's-back; & I fancied it might then be raining so hard at Chawton as to make you feel for us much more than we deserved.'

JANE TO CASSANDRA,
THURSDAY 20 MAY 1813

MOVING TO BATH

In May 1801, Jane moved to Bath with her parents and sister Cassandra. The move came after her father's sudden decision in December 1800 to retire and pass the Steventon living to his eldest son, James.

Reverend and Mrs Austen were excited for the move. Bath was a thriving spa resort and filled with amusements, even if, by 1801, it was past its fashionable best.

We don't know what Jane thought of life in Bath. We know that she loved dancing, shopping and going to the theatre, so it should have suited her well, but her letters suggest that she found the social circle tiresome and missed the Hampshire countryside.

Nevertheless, life in the city certainly gave her material for her novels. Bath features heavily in both *Northanger Abbey* and *Persuasion*. In *Northanger Abbey*, first drafted around 1798, before Jane's four-year sojourn in the city, Bath is shown through the eyes of Catherine Morland as a bustling city full of diversion. In *Persuasion*, written in Chawton in 1815–16, the depiction is much less positive. Anne Elliot dislikes Bath and dreads its 'white glare', while Bath society is shown to be vain and superficial.

'Upon Lady Russell's appearance soon afterwards, the whole party was collected, and all that remained was to marshal themselves, and proceed into the Concert Room; and be of all the consequence in their power, draw as many eyes, excite as many whispers, and disturb as many people as they could.'

PERSUASION, VOLUME II, CHAPTER 8

Wednesday. — I am just returned from my airing in the

[...]

very bewitching Phaeton & four, for which I was prepared by a note from M[...]

[...]

soon after breakfast: We went to the top of Kingsdown & had a very fine

[...]

drive: One pleasure succeeds another rapidly — On my return I found

[...]

letter & a little from Charles on the table. The contents of yours I sup[pose]

[...]

need not repeat to you; to thank you for it will be enough.

[...]

I give Charles great credit for remembering my Uncle's direction,

[...]

he seems rather surprised at it himself. — He has received 30£ for

[...]

share of the privateer & expects 10£ more — but of what avail i[s]

[...]

to take prizes if he lays out the produce in presents to his Sister

[...]

He has been buying gold chains & Topaze crosses for us; — he must

[...]

well scolded. — The Endymion has already received orders for taking

[...]

troops to Egypt — which I should not like at all if I did not tr[ust]

[...]

to Charles' being removed from her somehow or other before she sa[ils]

[...]

He knows nothing of his own destination he says, but desires m[e]

[...]

to write directly as the Endymion will probably sail in 30 days.

[...]

He will receive my yesterday's letter today, and I shall [...]

write again by this post to thank & reproach him. — We shall

unbearably fine. — I have made an engagement for you for Thursda[y]

of June; if my mother & Aunt should not go to the fireworks, which[...]

JANE TO CASSANDRA, TUESDAY 26 – WEDNESDAY 27 MAY 1801

Wednesday.—I am just returned from my Airing in the very bewitching Phaeton & four, for which I was prepared by a note from Mr E. soon after breakfast: We went to the top of Kingsdown—& had a very pleasant drive: One pleasure succeeds another rapidly—On my return I found your letter & a letter from Charles on the table. The contents of yours I suppose I need not repeat to you; to thank you for it will be enough.—I give Charles great credit for remembering my Uncle's direction, & he seems rather surprised at it himself.—He has received 30£ for his share of the privateer & expects 10£ more—but of what avail is it to take prizes if he lays out the produce in presents to his Sisters. He has been buying Gold chains & Topaze Crosses for us;—he must be well scolded.—The Endymion has already received orders for taking Troops to Egypt—which I should not like at all if I did not trust to Charles' being removed from her somehow or other before she sails. He knows nothing of his own destination he says,—but desires me to write directly, as the Endymion will probably sail in 3 or 4 days.—He will receive my yesterday's letter to day, and I shall write again by this post to thank & reproach him.—We shall be unbearably fine.—I have made an engagement for you for Thursday the 4th of June; if my Mother & Aunt should not go to the fireworks, which I dare say they will not, I have promised to join Mr Evelyn & Miss Wood—Miss Wood has lived with them you know ever "since my Son died—"

83

For economy, Jane turned back to the first page of her letter and wrote this section upside down, between the lines.

Transcript © Deirdre Le Faye, 2011, _Jane Austen's Letters._

PATCHWORK

This patchwork coverlet was made by Jane, Cassandra and their mother, at home in Chawton. We know they were working on a quilt (which may have been this one) in May 1811, as Jane mentioned it in a letter to Cassandra:

'Have you remembered to collect peices for the Patchwork?— We are now at a stand still.'

JANE TO CASSANDRA, FRIDAY 31 MAY 1811

Cassandra was staying at their brother Edward's estate of Godmersham in Kent, where there would have been many fabric pieces available from the dressmaker who made clothes for Edward's 11 children.

This quilt makes use of at least 64 fabrics, mostly block-printed dress weight fabrics as well as some roller printed textiles and furnishing fabrics. The intricate design was made using the English paper piecing method and was clearly carefully planned: it is perfectly symmetrical, with the top and bottom and left and right sides matching.

MOVING TO WINCHESTER

On 24 May 1817, having struggled with illness for over a year, Jane left Chawton with Cassandra and moved into lodgings in Winchester, to be near Dr Lyford at the County Hospital.

They took rooms at 8 College Street, a quiet street that backed on to the grounds of Winchester College and was close to the precincts of the Cathedral. Jane wrote:

'Our Lodgings are very comfortable. We have a neat little Draw^g -room with a Bow-window overlooking Dr Gabell's Garden.'

JANE TO HER NEPHEW JAMES EDWARD AUSTEN-LEIGH, TUESDAY 27 MAY 1817

Dr Henry Gabell was the headmaster of Winchester College at the time. His garden was surrounded by high walls that Jane and Cassandra could see over from their first-floor rooms.

Today, the house has a blue plaque to mark Jane's sojourn. Just a few doors up is P&G Wells – thought to be Britain's oldest bookshop – which has been operating at 11 College Street since 1789 and which Jane Austen is known to have visited.

THE 'TOPAZE CROSSES'

In May 1801 Jane's younger brother Charles, an officer in the Royal Navy, came into land in Portsmouth. He wrote to his family to tell of his good fortune – his ship had captured a French privateer, resulting in his earning £30 of prize money. With some of this largesse, he had bought his sisters each a topaz cross on a gold chain.

On 27 May, Jane wrote jokingly to Cassandra:

'of what avail is it to take prizes if he lays out the produce in presents to his Sisters. He has been buying Gold chains & Topaze Crosses for us;—he must be well scolded.'

A few years later, Jane wrote *Mansfield Park*, her third novel to be published. Its heroine, Fanny Price, has a sailor brother called William who, like Charles Austen, gives his sister a 'very pretty' amber cross. It is one of the rare occasions when we can see events in Jane's own life being worked into her novels.

THE JANE AUSTEN SOCIETY

The Jane Austen Society was founded in May 1940 by Miss Dorothy Darnell, an artist who lived in the Georgian market town of Alton, just over a mile from Chawton.

Dorothy was a lifelong admirer of Jane Austen and took an interest in the house she had lived in. Following the death of Cassandra Austen in 1845, the house had reverted to the Chawton estate. It was divided into three dwellings for estate workers, with the drawing room serving as a working men's club for the village. Over the next 100 years, as tenants came and went, it fell into disrepair.

On 2 January 1939, Dorothy visited Jane Austen's house, no doubt paying a small fee to one of the families living there, and was allowed to look around the building. She made some notes on the layout of the house and garden, concluding 'The view of the house ... gives the impression of a very perfect whole capable of being restored almost to its original state.' It seems she was already thinking

BELOW Jane Austen's House in the early twentieth century.

of rescuing the house and preserving it in Jane Austen's memory.

In 1940, Dorothy was walking past the house again when she was horrified to see the grate from the Dining Room lying on a heap of nettles by the neighbouring forge, having been removed to make way for a tenant's gas fire. She contacted the Curtis Museum in Alton who agreed to house the grate until it could be restored to its rightful place.

Dorothy then took matters into her own hands, forming the Jane Austen Society in May 1940 with the intention of raising £3000 to buy the house and a further £2000 to restore it and open it as a museum. She served as secretary of the society, a role shared with the novelist Elizabeth Jenkins, while her sister Beatrix served as the treasurer.

Today the Jane Austen Society continues to flourish, welcoming new members to the national society and regional branches and promoting awareness and appreciation of Jane Austen's life and works.

LEFT Before the house was opened as a museum, the drawing room was used as a club room for village labourers.

JUNE

'It was now the middle of June, and the weather fine.'

EMMA, VOLUME III, CHAPTER 6

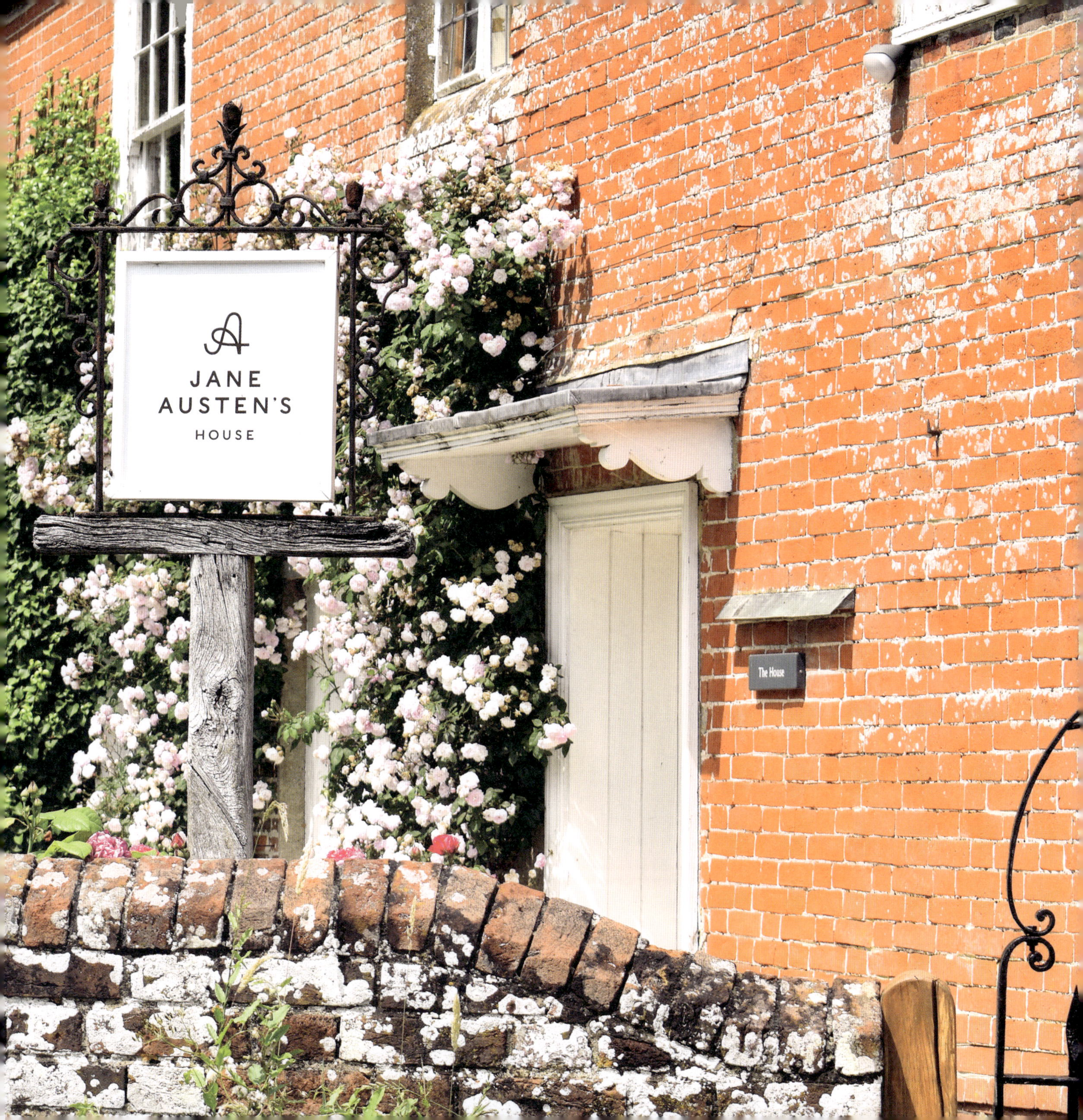
JANE
AUSTEN'S
HOUSE
The House

OXFORDSHIRE
MILITIA.
C. 1800.

96

MARY PEARSON

In 1796 Jane's brother Henry, who was serving as an Officer in the Oxfordshire Militia, became engaged to a Miss Mary Pearson, the daughter of a distinguished naval officer.

Jane met Mary while staying at Rowling in Kent and sent home a rather scathing opinion of her appearance, warning Cassandra 'pray be careful not to expect too much Beauty'. The Austens' cousin Eliza de Feuillide was also not keen on Mary (who, it must be noted, she never actually met), describing her as 'a most intolerable Flirt'.

The engagement did not last long and by the autumn it was broken off. Henry went to London and consoled himself with Eliza, whom he married in 1797, but poor Mary did not marry for nearly 20 years.

As a young, pretty girl who jumped into a short-lived engagement with a dashing young soldier, it has been suggested that Mary Pearson may have provided inspiration for the character of Lydia Bennet in *Pride and Prejudice*. While this cannot be proved, it is true that Jane began writing her militia novel *First Impressions* (later published as *Pride and Prejudice*) in the autumn of 1796, just as Henry and Mary's engagement was at the height of interest.

In *Pride and Prejudice* Jane noted the attraction of military men to vulnerable young women like Mary Pearson. Kitty and Lydia indeed 'could talk of nothing but officers; and Mr. Bingley's large fortune, the mention of which gave animation to their mother, was worthless in their eyes when opposed to the regimentals of an ensign.'

ABOVE
Coloured drawing of an officer in the Oxfordshire Militia c.1800, by Joan Corder.

OPPOSITE
Portrait miniature of Mary Pearson by William Wood, 1798.

'I can recollect
nothing more to say
at present;—perhaps
Breakfast may assist my
ideas. I was deceived—
my breakfast supplied
only two ideas, that the
rolls were good, & the
butter bad;—'

JANE TO CASSANDRA,
WEDNESDAY 19 JUNE 1799

99

THE PARTY TO BOX HILL

In Emma, *the ill-fated visit to Box Hill takes place on a hot day in June.*

They had a very fine day for Box Hill; and all the other outward circumstances of arrangement, accommodation, and punctuality, were in favour of a pleasant party. Mr. Weston directed the whole, officiating safely between Hartfield and the Vicarage, and every body was in good time. Emma and Harriet went together; Miss Bates and her niece, with the Eltons; the gentlemen on horseback. Mrs. Weston remained with Mr. Woodhouse. Nothing was wanting but to be happy when they got there. Seven miles were travelled in expectation of enjoyment, and every body had a burst of admiration on first arriving; but in the general amount of the day there was deficiency. There was a languor, a want of spirits, a want of union, which could not be got over. They separated too much into parties. The Eltons walked together; Mr. Knightley took charge of Miss Bates and Jane; and Emma and Harriet belonged to Frank Churchill. And Mr. Weston tried, in vain, to make them harmonise better. It seemed at first an accidental division, but it never materially varied. Mr. and Mrs. Elton, indeed, shewed no unwillingness to mix, and be as agreeable as they could; but during the two whole hours that were spent on the hill, there seemed a principle of separation, between the other parties, too strong for any fine prospects, or any cold collation, or any cheerful Mr. Weston, to remove.

At first it was downright dulness to Emma. She had never seen Frank Churchill so silent and stupid. He said nothing worth hearing—looked without seeing—admired without intelligence—listened without knowing what she said. While he was so dull, it was no wonder that Harriet should be dull likewise; and they were both insufferable.

When they all sat down it was better; to her taste a great deal better, for Frank Churchill grew talkative and gay, making her his first object. Every distinguishing attention that could be paid, was paid to her. To amuse her, and be agreeable in her eyes, seemed all that he cared for—and Emma, glad to be enlivened, not sorry to be flattered, was gay and easy too, and gave him all the friendly encouragement, the admission to be gallant, which she had ever given in the first and most animating period of their acquaintance; but which now, in her own estimation, meant nothing, though in the judgment of most people looking on it must have had such an appearance as no English word but flirtation could very well describe. "Mr. Frank Churchill and Miss Woodhouse flirted together excessively." They were laying themselves open to that very phrase—and to having it sent off in a letter to Maple Grove by one lady, to Ireland by another. Not that Emma was gay and thoughtless from any real felicity; it was rather because she felt less happy than she had expected. She laughed because she was disappointed; and though she liked him for his attentions, and thought them all, whether in friendship, admiration, or playfulness, extremely judicious, they were not winning back her heart. She still intended him for her friend.

EMMA, VOLUME III, CHAPTER 7

'Last night we were in Sidney Gardens again, as there was a repetition of the Gala which went off so ill on the 4th.—We did not go till nine, & then were in very good time for the Fire-works, which were really beautiful, & surpassing my expectation;—the illuminations too were very pretty.'

JANE TO CASSANDRA, WEDNESDAY 19 JUNE 1799

103

The Triumphal Arches, Mr. Handel's Statue & c. in the South Walk of Vauxhall Gardens, John S. Muller.

'You know how
interesting the
purchase of a
sponge-cake is
to me.'

JANE TO CASSANDRA,
FRIDAY 17 JUNE 1808

—
104

BLUSH NOISETTE

On the side wall of Jane Austen's House, a
wonderful Blush Noisette rose frames the door to
the kitchen and fills the drawing room with a heady
fragrance from June to September.

Blush Noisette is a short, compact climber that
produces masses of pale pink flowers. Growing
in tight clusters, the small, semi-double blooms
repeat freely throughout the summer and have a
distinctive clove fragrance.

Blush Noisette was developed in America in
the early nineteenth century and made its way to
Europe in 1817, the year of Jane Austen's death. It is
reputed to be the ancestor of most modern garden
hybrid roses.

JULY

'July begins
unpleasantly with us,
cold & showery, but
it is often a baddish
month. We had some
fine dry weather
preceding it, which was
very acceptable to the
Holders of Hay & the
Masters of Meadows—
In general it must
have been a good
Haymaking Season.'

JANE TO FRANK AUSTEN,
SATURDAY 3 JULY 1813

111

MOVING TO CHAWTON

In 1809, Jane's brother Edward offered his mother and sisters the free use of a house on one of his estates. This was possible because Edward had been adopted as heir to the Austen's distant, wealthy relatives, Mr and Mrs Knight, and inherited their estates of Chawton and Steventon in Hampshire and Godmersham in Kent.

The Austen women chose the house in Chawton. It was a modest house, particularly when compared with Edward's vast estates, but it was pretty and comfortable. It had its origins in the late fifteenth century when it was built as a timber-framed dwelling for use as a farmhouse; over the next few centuries it was extended and became known as 'Petty Johns'. It was incorporated into the Chawton estate in 1769 and for a while it was used as a pub, and then as the Bailiff's house for the estate.

Before his mother and sisters moved in, Edward Austen made some improvements, including bricking up a window that looked straight onto the busy road and cutting a new one that overlooked the garden.

The Austen women moved in on 7 July 1809 with their friend Martha Lloyd, who had previously lived with them in Southampton. Together they formed a stable and comfortable female household.

Mrs Austen threw her energies into working in the garden, while Cassandra and Martha took over the household management, leaving Jane to focus on her writing. For the first time since her childhood in Steventon, she had a settled home and the space and time in which to focus on her work, and she began in earnest – taking out her early draft novel *Elinor and Marianne* and revising it for publication as *Sense and Sensibility*.

JANE TO FRANK AUSTEN, 26 JULY 1809

My dearest Frank, I wish you Joy
Of Mary's safety with a boy,
Whose birth has given little pain,
Compared with that of Mary Jane.–
May he a growing Blessing prove,
And well deserve his Parents Love!
Endow'd with Art's & Nature's Good,
Thy name possessing with thy Blood;
In him, in all his ways, may we
Another Francis William see!–
Thy infant days may he inherit,
Thy warmth, nay insolence of spirit;–
We would not with one fault dispense
To weaken the resemblance.
May he revive thy Nursery sin,
Peeping as daringly within,
(His curley Locks but just descried)
With, "Bet, my be not come to bide."
Fearless of danger, braving pain,
And threaten'd very oft in vain,
Still may one Terror daunt his soul
One needful engine of controul
Be found in this sublime array,
A neigbouring Donkey's aweful Bray!–
So may his equal faults as Child
Produce Maturity as mild,
His saucy words & fiery ways
In early Childhood's pettish days

Copy of a letter to Frank, July 26. 1809.

In Manhood shew his Father's mind,
Like him considerate & kind;
All Gentleness to those around,
And eager only not to wound.
Then like his Father too, he must,
To his own former struggles just,
Feel his Deserts with honest Glow,
And all his Self-improvement know.—
A native fault may thus give birth
To the best blessing, conscious worth.—
    As for ourselves, we're very well,
As unaffected prose will tell.
Cassandra's pen will give our state
The many comforts that await
Our Chawton home — how much we find
Already in it to our mind,
And how convinced that when complete,
It will all other Houses beat,
That ever have been made or mended,
With rooms concise or rooms distended.
    You'll find us very snug next year;
Perhaps with Charles & Fanny near—
For now it often does delight us
To fancy them just over-right us.

J.A.

Transcript © Deirdre Le Faye, 2011, *Jane Austen's Letters*.

JANE AUSTEN'S DEATH

Jane Austen died in the early hours of Thursday 18 July 1817. She was just 41 years old and had been struggling with illness for over a year. We do not know for sure what she died of; various theories have been suggested including Addison's disease, Hodgkin's lymphoma or the autoimmune condition lupus erythematosus. Since all that modern physicians have to go on are the symptoms mentioned in Jane's letters, it is unlikely that we will ever know for sure.

On 20 July, Cassandra wrote to her niece, Fanny Knight, describing Jane's last hours:

'Since Tuesday evening,
when her complaint returnd,
there was a visible change,
she slept more & much more
comfortably, indeed, during the
last eight & forty hours she was
more asleep than awake. Her
looks altered & she fell away,
but I perceived no material
diminution of strength & tho' I
was then hopeless of a recovery
I had no suspicion how rapidly
my loss was approaching.—I
have lost a treasure, such a
Sister, such a friend as never
can have been surpassed,—
She was the sun of my life, the
gilder of every pleasure, the
soother of every sorrow, I had
not a thought concealed from
her, & it is as if I had lost a part
of myself.'

Jane was buried in Winchester Cathedral on 24 July. Her modest funeral took place early in the morning, before services began, and was attended by just four people – her brothers Henry, Edward and Frank, and her nephew James Edward.

Her tombstone, set in the floor of the north aisle of the Cathedral, refers to 'the extraordinary endowments of her mind', but makes no mention of her writing.

PEMBERLEY

In Pride and Prejudice, *Lizzy and the Gardiners visit Pemberley in July, while they are touring the Lake District.*

Watercolour painting of Godmersham Park by William Watts c.1780.

Elizabeth, as they drove along, watched for the first appearance of Pemberley Woods with some perturbation; and when at length they turned in at the lodge, her spirits were in a high flutter.

The park was very large, and contained great variety of ground. They entered it in one of its lowest points, and drove for some time through a beautiful wood stretching over a wide extent.

Elizabeth's mind was too full for conversation, but she saw and admired every remarkable spot and point of view. They gradually ascended for half-a-mile, and then found themselves at the top of a considerable eminence, where the wood ceased, and the eye was instantly caught by Pemberley House, situated on the opposite side of a valley, into which the road with some abruptness wound. It was a large, handsome stone building, standing well on rising ground, and backed by a ridge of high woody hills; and in front, a stream of some natural importance was swelled into greater, but without any artificial appearance. Its banks were neither formal nor falsely adorned. Elizabeth was delighted. She had never seen a place for which nature had done more, or where natural beauty had been so little counteracted by an awkward taste. They were all of them warm in their admiration; and at that moment she felt that to be mistress of Pemberley might be something!

They descended the hill, crossed the bridge, and drove to the door; and, while examining the nearer aspect of the house, all her apprehension of meeting its owner returned. She dreaded lest the chambermaid had been mistaken. On applying to see the place, they were admitted into the hall; and Elizabeth, as they waited for the housekeeper, had leisure to wonder at her being where she was.

The housekeeper came; a respectable-looking elderly woman, much less fine, and more civil, than she had any notion of finding her. They followed her into the dining-parlour. It was a large, well proportioned room, handsomely fitted up. Elizabeth, after slightly surveying it, went to a window to enjoy its prospect. The hill, crowned with wood, which they had descended, receiving increased abruptness from the distance, was a beautiful object. Every disposition of the ground was good; and she looked on the whole scene, the river, the trees scattered on its banks and the winding of the valley, as far as she could trace it, with delight. As they passed into other rooms these objects were taking different positions; but from every window there were beauties to be seen. The rooms were lofty and handsome, and their furniture suitable to the fortune of its proprietor; but Elizabeth saw, with admiration of his taste, that it was neither gaudy nor uselessly fine; with less of splendour, and more real elegance, than the furniture of Rosings.

'And of this place,' thought she, 'I might have been mistress! With these rooms I might now have been familiarly acquainted! Instead of viewing them as a stranger, I might have rejoiced in them as my own, and welcomed to them as visitors my uncle and aunt. But no,'—recollecting herself—'that could never be; my uncle and aunt would have been lost to me; I should not have been allowed to invite them.'

This was a lucky recollection—it saved her from something very like regret.

PRIDE AND PREJUDICE, VOLUME III, CHAPTER 1

OPENING OF JANE AUSTEN'S HOUSE

Throughout the 1940s, the Jane Austen Society endeavoured to raise enough money to buy the house in Chawton where Jane Austen had lived, to preserve it for the nation. In 1946 they put a notice in *The Times* calling for donations. This caught the attention of Mr T. Edward Carpenter, a London lawyer, who in 1948 purchased the house in memory of his son Philip who had been killed in action in 1944. He established the Jane Austen Memorial Trust to run the house as a museum.

Jane Austen's House was opened to the public on 23 July 1949. Members of the Jane Austen Society gathered in a nearby marquee for their annual meeting before crowding into the cottage garden to watch the Duke of Wellington declare the museum officially open.

At the time, only the drawing room was open to visitors as the rest of the house was still occupied by tenants. Over the years, as the tenants moved out, more rooms were opened to the public.

DRESS UP DAY

In July each year, Jane Austen's House hosts an annual Dress Up Day, encouraging visitors to attend in Regency outfits. With talks and demonstrations, posing and photographs, Dress Up Day has quickly become one of the most popular days of the year. It's an opportunity to meet like-minded Austen aficionados, enjoy the elegance of a bygone age and feel like you are stepping into the pages of an Austen novel!

'I never in my life saw anything more elegant than their dresses.'

PRIDE AND PREJUDICE,
VOLUME I, CHAPTER 3

JANE AUSTEN GOES TO HOLLYWOOD

MGM's lavish adaptation of *Pride and Prejudice*, starring Laurence Olivier and Greer Garson, opened in cinemas on 26 July 1940.

The film received both high praise and disparaging criticism. *The New York Times* praised it as 'the most deliciously pert comedy of old manners, the most crisp and crackling satire in costume that we in this corner can remember ever having seen on the screen', while others derided its extraordinary costumes and divergences from Jane Austen's lines and plot.

LEFT Portrait still of Greer Garson and Laurence Olivier in *Pride and Prejudice* (1940).

LEFT Alicia
Silverstone
starred in *Clueless*
(1995).

123

EMMA IN L.A.

On 19 July 1995, Amy Heckerling's
teen movie *Clueless* burst onto
American cinema screens. The
plot was based on Jane Austen's
Emma, with a modern-day setting
of Beverly Hills. Alicia Silverstone
played the central character, Cher –
a rich, beautiful high school student
who enjoyed shopping, makeovers
and playing matchmaker.

Clueless was a surprise hit at the
box office, developed a cult following,
and is still considered to be one of
the best teen films of all time.

AUGUST

SOTHERTON

In Mansfield Park, *the fateful visit to Sotherton takes place on a hot day in August.*

Illustration for
Mansfield Park, by
Joan Hassall (Folio
Society, 1961).

After a moment's embarrassment the lady replied, 'You are too much a man of the world not to see with the eyes of the world. If other people think Sotherton improved, I have no doubt that you will.'

'I am afraid I am not quite so much the man of the world as might be good for me in some points. My feelings are not quite so evanescent, nor my memory of the past under such easy dominion as one finds to be the case with men of the world.'

This was followed by a short silence. Miss Bertram began again. 'You seemed to enjoy your drive here very much this morning. I was glad to see you so well entertained. You and Julia were laughing the whole way.'

'Were we? Yes, I believe we were; but I have not the least recollection at what. Oh! I believe I was relating to her some ridiculous stories of an old Irish groom of my uncle's. Your sister loves to laugh.'

'You think her more light-hearted than I am?'

'More easily amused,' he replied; 'consequently, you know,' smiling, 'better company. I could not have hoped to entertain you with Irish anecdotes during a ten miles' drive.'

'Naturally, I believe, I am as lively as Julia, but I have more to think of now.'

'You have, undoubtedly; and there are situations in which very high spirits would denote insensibility. Your prospects, however, are too fair to justify want of spirits. You have a very smiling scene before you.'

'Do you mean literally or figuratively? Literally, I conclude. Yes, certainly, the sun shines, and the park looks very cheerful. But unluckily that iron gate, that ha-ha, give me a feeling of restraint and hardship. "I cannot get out," as the starling said.' As she spoke, and it was with expression, she walked to the gate: he followed her. 'Mr. Rushworth is so long fetching this key!'

'And for the world you would not get out without the key and without Mr. Rushworth's authority and protection, or I think you might with little difficulty pass round the edge of the gate, here, with my assistance; I think it might be done, if you really wished to be more at large, and could allow yourself to think it not prohibited.'

'Prohibited! nonsense! I certainly can get out that way, and I will. Mr. Rushworth will be here in a moment, you know; we shall not be out of sight.'

'Or if we are, Miss Price will be so good as to tell him that he will find us near that knoll: the grove of oak on the knoll.'

Fanny, feeling all this to be wrong, could not help making an effort to prevent it. 'You will hurt yourself, Miss Bertram,' she cried; "you will certainly hurt yourself against those spikes; you will tear your gown; you will be in danger of slipping into the ha-ha. You had better not go.'

Her cousin was safe on the other side while these words were spoken, and, smiling with all the good-humour of success, she said, 'Thank you, my dear Fanny, but I and my gown are alive and well, and so good-bye.'

Fanny was again left to her solitude, and with no increase of pleasant feelings, for she was sorry for almost all that she had seen and heard, astonished at Miss Bertram, and angry with Mr. Crawford. By taking a circuitous, and, as it appeared to her, very unreasonable direction to the knoll, they were soon beyond her eye; and for some minutes longer she remained without sight or sound of any companion. She seemed to have the little wood all to herself. She could almost have thought that Edmund and Miss Crawford had left it, but that it was impossible for Edmund to forget her so entirely.

MANSFIELD PARK, VOLUME I, CHAPTER 10

LANDSCAPE GARDENING

Humphry Repton was one of the great landscape gardeners of the eighteenth century, designing some 300 estates in his signature style that broke down the division between garden and countryside.

He produced beautifully illustrated 'Red Books' for his clients, using flaps of paper to show the landscape in its original state with his proposed new design underneath.

This design for Brandsbury in Middlesex shows one of the first estates that Repton 'improved'. In this case, a fence was removed to open up the view of picturesque rolling meadows. The image

of a gentleman and two ladies peering through the fence is perfectly reminiscent of *Mansfield Park*, in which the Misses Bertram and Mr Crawford climb over a fence to gain access to the wider parkland on their day out to Sotherton.

Designs by Humphry Repton, *Sketches and Hints on Landscape Gardening* (1795). The white flap on the side of the picture is attached to the fence, which can be lifted to reveal the improved landscape behind it.

TOASTED CHEESE

On 26 August 1805, Jane Austen had cheese on toast for dinner. We know this because the next day she wrote to Cassandra and made particular mention of it, recounting that she had dined with their friend Edward Brydges:

'**It is impossible to do justice to the hospitality of his attentions towards me; he made a point of ordering toasted cheese for supper entirely on my account.**'

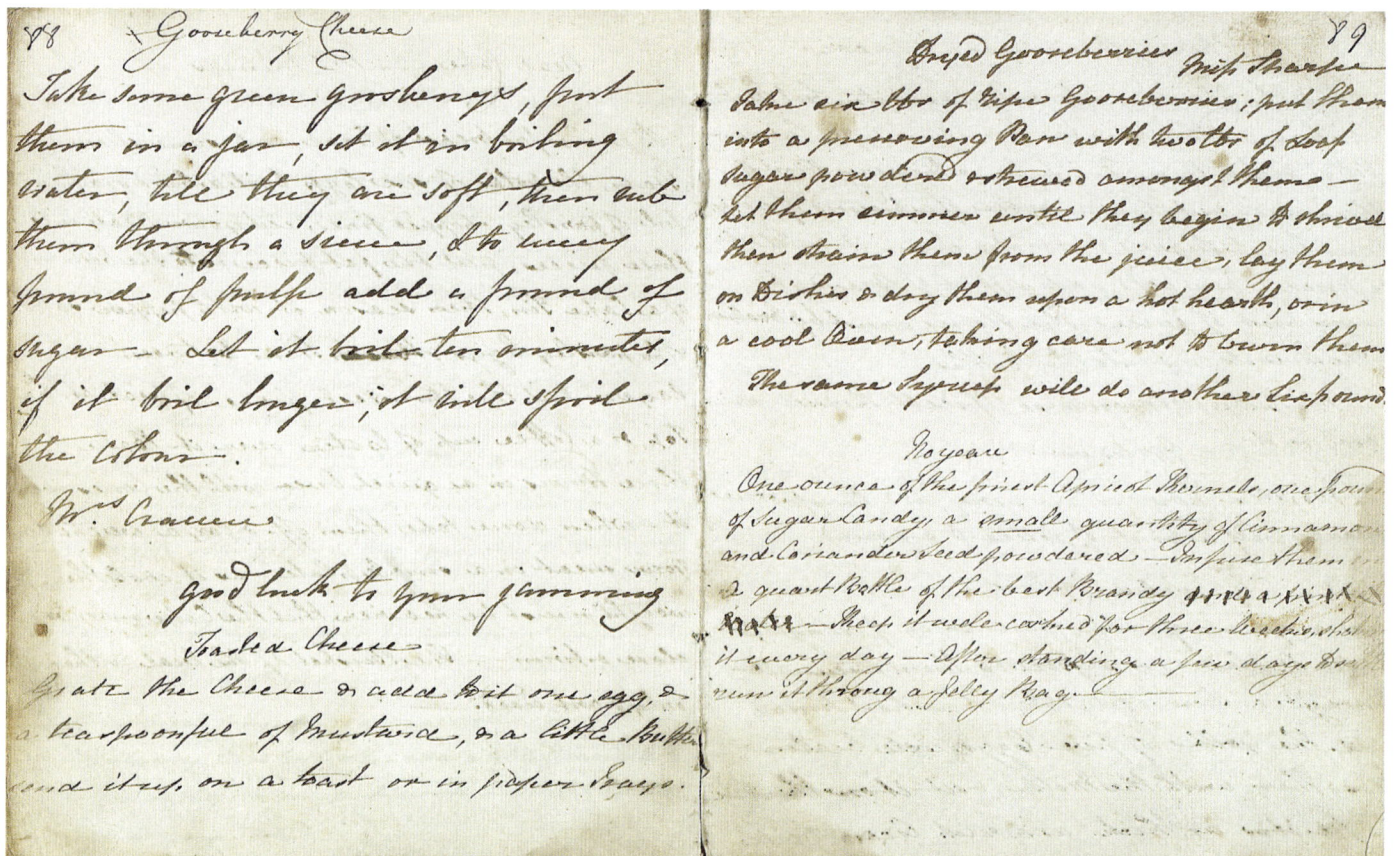

Jane's toasted cheese would have been rather like a modern Welsh Rarebit, with a cheesy custard spread on toast and grilled until brown and bubbling.

Jane's friend Martha Lloyd recorded a recipe for it in her *Household Book*:

'Grate the Cheese & add to it one egg, & a teaspoonful of Mustard, & a little Butter send it up on a toast or in paper Trays.'

Above the recipe, on the same page, is a recipe for Gooseberry Cheese – a rich, fruity preserve. This would have been another good recipe to make in August, when the gooseberries in Mrs Austen's garden would have been ripe and luscious.

UPPERCROSS

In Persuasion *we know from the Baronetage, Sir Walter Elliot's favourite book, that Anne Elliot's birthday is 9 August. This is also the month that sees the break-up of Kellynch, with Sir Walter and Elizabeth removing to Bath and Anne to Uppercross.*

Amanda Root starred in *Persuasion* (1995).

Her friend was not in better spirits than herself. Lady Russell felt this break-up of the family exceedingly. Their respectability was as dear to her as her own, and a daily intercourse had become precious by habit. It was painful to look upon their deserted grounds, and still worse to anticipate the new hands they were to fall into; and to escape the solitariness and the melancholy of so altered a village, and be out of the way when Admiral and Mrs Croft first arrived, she had determined to make her own absence from home begin when she must give up Anne. Accordingly their removal was made together, and Anne was set down at Uppercross Cottage, in the first stage of Lady Russell's journey.

Uppercross was a moderate-sized village, which a few years back had been completely in the old English style, containing only two houses superior in appearance to those of the yeomen and labourers; the mansion of the squire, with its high walls, great gates, and old trees, substantial and unmodernized, and the compact, tight parsonage, enclosed in its own neat garden, with a vine and a pear-tree trained round its casements; but upon the marriage of the young 'squire, it had received the improvement of a farm-house elevated into a cottage, for his residence, and Uppercross Cottage, with its veranda, French windows, and other prettiness, was quite as likely to catch the traveller's eye as the more consistent and considerable aspect and premises of the Great House, about a quarter of a mile farther on.

Here Anne had often been staying. She knew the ways of Uppercross as well as those of Kellynch. The two families were so continually meeting, so much in the habit of running in and out of each other's house at all hours, that it was rather a surprise to her to find Mary alone; but being alone, her being unwell and out of spirits was almost a matter of course. Though better endowed than the elder sister, Mary had not Anne's understanding nor temper. While well, and happy, and properly attended to, she had great good humour and excellent spirits; but any indisposition sunk her completely. She had no resources for solitude; and inheriting a considerable share of the Elliot self-importance, was very prone to add to every other distress that of fancying herself neglected and ill-used. In person, she was inferior to both sisters, and had, even in her bloom, only reached the dignity of being 'a fine girl.' She was now lying on the faded sofa of the pretty little drawing-room, the once elegant furniture of which had been gradually growing shabby, under the influence of four summers and two children; and, on Anne's appearing, greeted her with--

'So, you are come at last! I began to think I should never see you. I am so ill I can hardly speak.

I have not seen a creature the whole morning!'

'I am sorry to find you unwell,' replied Anne. 'You sent me such a good account of yourself on Thursday!'

'Yes, I made the best of it; I always do: but I was very far from well at the time; and I do not think I ever was so ill in my life as I have been all this morning: very unfit to be left alone, I am sure. Suppose I were to be seized of a sudden in some dreadful way, and not able to ring the bell! So, Lady Russell would not get out. I do not think she has been in this house three times this summer.'

PERSUASION, VOLUME I, CHAPTER 5

HANDKERCHIEFS

This handkerchief was worked by Jane Austen for her sister Cassandra. It is embroidered in satin stitch with a floral sprig and the initials 'C.A.' in one corner.

We know that Jane gave another gift of handkerchiefs in 1808, this time to her friend Catherine Bigg as a wedding present. She composed a few lines of verse to accompany them:

Cambrick! with grateful
blessings would I pay
The pleasure given me in
sweet employ:—
Long may'st thou serve my
Friend without decay,
And have no tears to wipe,
but tears of joy!—

J.A. AUG 26. 1808

Three of the Bigg sisters – Alethea, Elizabeth and Catherine – were close friends of Jane and Cassandra. They lived at Manydown Park, about two and a half miles from Steventon.

In 1802, Jane and Cassandra were staying at Manydown when Jane received an offer of marriage from their friends' brother, Harris Bigg-Wither. She accepted him, but the following morning she changed her mind and retracted her acceptance; she and Cassandra left the house at once.

134

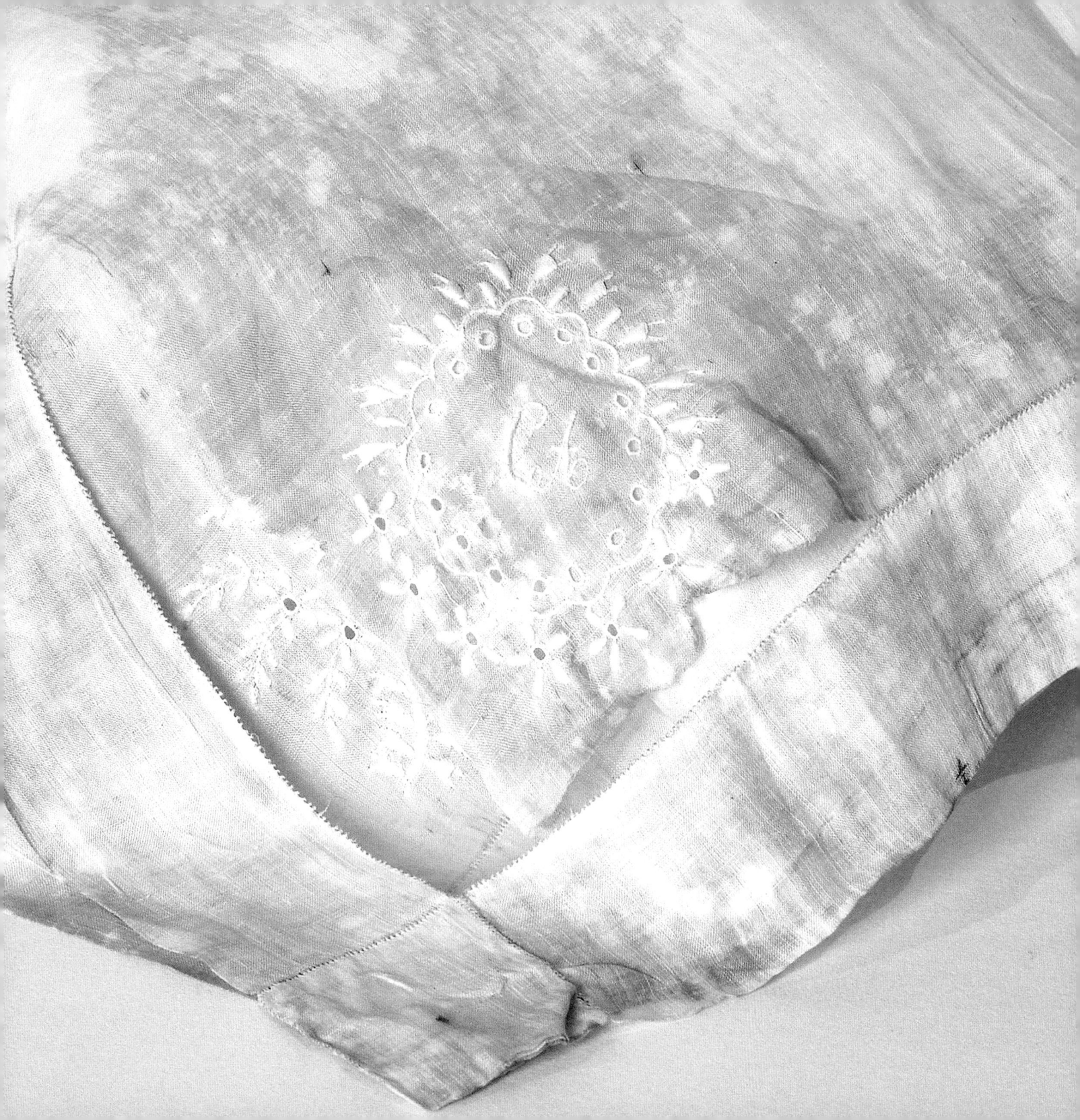

STONELEIGH ABBEY

In August 1806, Jane and her mother paid a visit to Stoneleigh Abbey in Warwickshire, the ancestral home of their relatives, the Leighs. The last occupier of the Abbey had just died and Mrs Austen's cousin, Reverend Thomas Leigh, was the principal claimant to inherit. He moved into the Abbey without delay, taking with him his sister, lawyer and entire house party, including the Austens.

Mrs Austen documented the visit in a letter to her daughter-in-law, Mary Lloyd, written on 13 August 1806:

'...here we found ourselves on Tuesday (that is yesterday se'nnight) eating fish, venison, and all manner of good things, in a large and noble parlour, hung round with family portraits. The house is larger than I could have supposed. We cannot find our way about it – I mean the best part; as to the offices, which were the Abbey, Mr. Leigh almost despairs of ever finding his way about them. I have proposed his setting up direction posts at the angles. I had expected to find everything about the place very fine and all that, but I had no idea of its being so beautiful. I had pictured to myself long avenues, dark rookeries, and dismal yew trees, but here are no such dismal things. The Avon runs near the house, amidst green meadows, bounded by large and beautiful woods, full of delightful walks.'

She went on to describe everything from the breakfast ('chocolate, coffee, and tea, plum cake, pound cake, hot rolls, cold rolls, bread and butter and dry toast for me') to the chapel, which is thought to have been Jane's model for the chapel at Sotherton in *Mansfield Park*.

LAVENDER

In the summer months, the Austen women would have picked fragrant bunches of lavender for all sorts of household uses. Lavender oil was used to treat burns and ward off infection, while a cold compress of lavender water was used to bring down a fever.

Many Regency ladies would carry a small bottle of lavender water with them to sniff if they felt anxious or faint, just as they would smelling salts.

At home, lavender water was sprinkled onto bed linens and undergarments to keep them smelling fresh, and sachets of dried lavender flowers were stored with clean linens to help repel insects.

'Marianne, now looking dreadfully white, and unable to stand, sunk into her chair, and Elinor, expecting every moment to see her faint, tried to screen her from the observation of others, while reviving her with lavender water.'

SENSE AND SENSIBILITY, VOLUME II, CHAPTER 6

SEPTEMBER

SEASIDE HOLIDAYS

September was a time for holidays. The Austens particularly enjoyed visits to the seaside and between 1801–9, while they were living in Bath and Southampton, they visited Dawlish, Teignmouth, Sidmouth, Worthing, Lyme Regis and possibly Barmouth and Tenby. These holidays were an opportunity to escape the dirt and crowds of the city and to enjoy space, quiet coastal walks, sea bathing and fresh air.

Jane herself never learned to swim, but she delighted in sea bathing. Under the guidance of a bathing woman or 'dipper', she could splash around in the water, enjoying the bodily pleasure of floating on or being buffeted by the waves. Like dancing, sea bathing offered a rare sense of physical freedom that she relished.

Seaside holidays are also renowned for romance. Jane may have experienced a seaside romance of her own in the summer of 1801, although sadly we do not know exactly what happened as no letters from this period survive. A family story maintains that she met a young man, possibly at Sidmouth, possibly a clergyman. He had to leave to fulfil another engagement, but promised to return; however they then heard the tragedy that he had died.

Other holiday romances occur in the novels. In *Pride and Prejudice* Lydia Bennet and Wickham elope from Brighton, and in *Persuasion* Louisa Musgrove finds love with Captain Benwick during her convalescence in Lyme. Anne herself is restored to 'the bloom and freshness of youth' by Lyme's 'fine wind' and catches the eye of Mr Elliot while walking on the Cobb, which Captain Wentworth notices at once:

'Captain Wentworth looked round at her instantly in a way which shewed his noticing of it. He gave her a momentary glance,—a glance of brightness, which seemed to say, 'That man is struck with you,— and even I, at this moment, see something like Anne Elliot again.'

PERSUASION, VOLUME I, CHAPTER 12

ABOVE Women swimming in the sea at Brighton. Coloured etching by W. Heath.

OPPOSITE Illustration by Hugh Thomson for *Persuasion* (Macmillan and Co., 1897).

'What dreadful Hot weather we have!—It keeps one in a continual state of Inelegance.'

JANE TO CASSANDRA,
SUNDAY 18 SEPTEMBER 1796

Lyme Regis, seen
from the Cobb.

MEETING WILLOUGHBY

In Sense and Sensibility, *the Dashwoods move to Barton 'very early in September'. A few weeks later, Marianne and Margaret go out for an eventful walk in the hills near their cottage.*

Kate Winslet and Greg Wise starred in *Sense and Sensibility* (1995).

The whole country about them abounded in beautiful walks. The high downs which invited them from almost every window of the cottage to seek the exquisite enjoyment of air on their summits, were a happy alternative when the dirt of the valleys beneath shut up their superior beauties; and towards one of these hills did Marianne and Margaret one memorable morning direct their steps, attracted by the partial sunshine of a showery sky, and unable longer to bear the confinement which the settled rain of the two preceding days had occasioned. The weather was not tempting enough to draw the two others from their pencil and their book, in spite of Marianne's declaration that the day would be lastingly fair, and that every threatening cloud would be drawn off from their hills; and the two girls set off together.

They gaily ascended the downs, rejoicing in their own penetration at every glimpse of blue sky; and when they caught in their faces the animating gales of a high south-westerly wind, they pitied the fears which had prevented their mother and Elinor from sharing such delightful sensations.

'Is there a felicity in the world,' said Marianne, 'superior to this?—Margaret, we will walk here at least two hours.'

Margaret agreed, and they pursued their way against the wind, resisting it with laughing delight for about twenty minutes longer, when suddenly the clouds united over their heads, and a driving rain set full in their face. Chagrined and surprised, they were obliged, though unwillingly, to turn back, for no shelter was nearer than their own house. One consolation however remained for them, to which the exigence of the moment gave more than usual propriety,—it was that of running with all possible speed down the steep side of the hill which led immediately to their garden gate.

They set off. Marianne had at first the advantage, but a false step brought her suddenly to the ground; and Margaret, unable to stop herself to assist her, was involuntarily hurried along, and reached the bottom in safety.

A gentleman carrying a gun, with two pointers playing round him, was passing up the hill and within a few yards of Marianne, when her accident happened. He put down his gun and ran to her assistance. She had raised herself from the ground, but her foot had been twisted in her fall, and she was scarcely able to stand. The gentleman offered his services; and perceiving that her modesty declined what her situation rendered necessary, took her up in his arms without farther delay, and carried her down the hill. Then passing through the garden, the gate of which had been left open by Margaret, he bore her directly into the house, whither Margaret was just arrived, and quitted not his hold till he had seated her in a chair in the parlour.

Elinor and her mother rose up in amazement at their entrance, and while the eyes of both were fixed on him with an evident wonder and a secret admiration which equally sprung from his appearance, he apologized for his intrusion by relating its cause, in a manner so frank and so graceful that his person, which was uncommonly handsome, received additional charms from his voice and expression. Had he been even old, ugly, and vulgar, the gratitude and kindness of Mrs. Dashwood would have been secured by any act of attention to her child; but the influence of youth, beauty, and elegance, gave an interest to the action which came home to her feelings.

She thanked him again and again; and, with a sweetness of address which always attended her, invited him to be seated. But this he declined, as he was dirty and wet. Mrs. Dashwood then begged to know to whom she was obliged. His name, he replied, was Willoughby, and his present home was at Allenham, from whence he hoped she would allow him the honour of calling tomorrow to enquire after Miss Dashwood. The honour was readily granted, and he then departed, to make himself still more interesting, in the midst of a heavy rain.

SENSE AND SENSIBILITY, VOLUME I, CHAPTER 9

JANE TO CASSANDRA, 15–16 SEPTEMBER 1813

Henrietta St. Wednesday–½ past 8–

Here I am my dearest Cassandra, seated in the Breakfast, Dining, sitting room, beginning with all my might. Fanny will join me as soon as she is dressed & begin her Letter.–We had a very good Journey–Weather & roads excellent–the three first stages for 1ˢ 6ᵈ & our only misadventure the being delayed about a qʳ. of an hour at Kingston for Horses, & being obliged to put up with a pʳ. belonging to a Hackney Coach & their Coachman, which left no room on the Barouche Box for Lizzy, who was to have gone her last stage there, as she did the first;–consequently we were all 4 within, which was a little crowd.–We arrived at a qʳ. past 4–& were kindly welcomed by the Coachman, & then by his Master, & then by Wᵐ, & then by Mʳˢ. Perigord, who all met us before we reached the foot of the Stairs.–Mᵈᵉ. Bigeon was below dressing us a most comfortable dinner of Soup, Fish, Bouillée, Partridges & an apple Tart, which we sat down to soon after 5, after cleaning & dressing ourselves & feeling that we were most commodiously disposed of.–The little adjoining Dressing-room to our apartment makes Fanny & myself very well off indeed, & as we have poor Eliza's bed, our space is ample every way.–Sace arrived safely about ½ past 6.–At 7 we set off in a Coach for the Lyceum–were at home again in about 4 hours & ½–had soup & wine & water, & then went to our Holes.–Edward finds his quarters very snug & quiet.–I must get a softer pen.–This is harder. I am in agonies.–I have not yet seen Mʳ. Crabbe.–Martha's Letter is gone to the Post.–

I am going to write nothing but short Sentences. There shall be two full stops in every Line.–Layton & Shears is Bedford House. We mean to get there before Breakfast.–(if it's possible.)–For we feel more & more how much we have to do. And how little ^Time. This House looks very nice.–It seems like Sloane Sᵗ. moved here. I beleive Henry is just rid of Sloane Sᵗ.–Fanny does not come, but I have Edward seated by me, beginning a Letter, which looks natural.–Henry has been suffering from the pain in the face which he has been subject to before. He caught cold at Matlock, & since his return has been paying a little for past pleasure.–It is nearly removed now–but he looks thin in the face–either from the pain, or the fatigues of his Tour, which must have been great.–Lady Robert is delighted with P&P–& really <u>was</u> so as I understand before she knew who wrote it–for of course she knows now.–He told her with as much satisfaction as if it were my wish.–He did not tell <u>me</u> this, but he told Fanny.–And Mʳ. Hastings– I am quite delighted with what such a Man writes about it.–Henry sent him the Books after his return from Daylesford–but you will hear the Letter too.– Let me be rational & return to my two full stops. I talked to Henry at the Play last night.–We were in a private Box.–Mʳ. Spencer's.–Which made it much more pleasant.–The Box is directly on the Stage.–One is infinitely less fatigued than in the common way.

, sitting room, beginning with all my might. Fanny will jo[in]
as soon as she is dressed & begin her Letter. — We had a very g[ood jour]
ney — weather & roads excellent — the three first Stages for 1 — [&]
[o]ur only misadventure the being delayed about a qr. of an hour a[t]
[Kin]gston, for Horses, & being obliged to put up with a pr. belongin[g]
[to] a Hackney Coach & their Coachman, which left no room on the
[C]oach Box for Lizzy, who was to have gone her last stage th[ere as]
she did the first; — consequently we were all 4 within, whi[ch]
[was] a little crowd. — We arrived at a qr. past 4 — & were kind[ly]
[wel]comed by the Coachman, & then by his Master, & then by W[illiam]
[the]n by Mrs. Perigord, who all met us before we reached the[doo]r, [&]
[in] the Stairs. — Mde. Bigeon was below dressing us a most comfort[able]
[Din]ner of Soup, Fish, Bouillée, Partridges & an apple Tart, which we [sat]
[down] to soon after 5, after cleaning & dressing ourselves & fee[ling]
[tha]t we were most commodiously disposed of. — The little adjoin[ing]
[Din]ing-room to our apartment makes Fanny & myself very we[ll off]
indeed, & as we have poor Eliza's bed, our Space is ample
[ever]y way. — Sace arrived safely about ½ past 6. At 7 we
[set] off in a Coach for the Lyceum — were at home again in abo[ut]
[4 hou]rs & ½ — had Soup & wine & water, & then went to ou[r]
[be]ds. Edward finds his Quarters very sweet & quiet. — I mu[st]

HARVEST

September is a time for harvesting and preserving, building up supplies for the winter. *Martha Lloyd's Household Book* is full of recipes for fruit vinegars, cheeses and chutneys, including this one for raspberry vinegar, courtesy of their friend Mrs Lefroy:

Raspberry Vinegar

Put two quarts of large fine Rasberries into one quart of the best Vin'gar, let it stand 10 days near a fire, clarify 2 p^{ds} of fine Sugar, strain off the juice from the Rasberries, add the clarified Syrup & boil all together 'till it is fine — When it is cold put it into small Bottles & use it as you would Orgeat, mix it with Water to your taste — Mrs. Lefroy

'We hear now that there is to be <u>no Honey</u> this year. Bad news for us.—We must husband our present stock of Mead;'

JANE TO CASSANDRA,
MONDAY 9 SEPTEMBER 1816

REGENCY REVELS

Every September the streets of Bath are filled
with Regency revellers, as the Jane Austen Festival
takes over the city.

    Visitors to the festival enjoy walks, talks,
balls and performances, against the beautiful
backdrop of the Georgian city of Bath. The
highlight of the festival is the Regency Costumed
Promenade, which attracts over 500 people in
Regency dress and holds the Guinness World
Record for the 'Largest gathering of people
dressed in Regency costumes'.

AUSTEN-MANIA

In September 1995, Andrew Davies's sumptuous adaptation of *Pride and Prejudice* for the BBC burst onto British TV screens to critical acclaim and huge popularity. The six-part drama was screened weekly, attracting huge audiences. The press called it 'Austen-mania'. 100,000 video box sets were sold while the show was still on air, and 10 million people tuned in to watch the final episode.

Jennifer Ehle's portrayal of Elizabeth Bennet, the darling of English literature, was applauded, but it was Colin Firth's portrayal of Mr Darcy that caught the public imagination. The scene in which he emerges from a lake in a wet shirt has become one of the most iconic moments in British TV history – despite it not appearing in the novel – and the shirt itself has taken on a cult status. In 2024 one of the shirts used in filming this scene was sold at a charity auction for £25,000, making it surely the most expensive piece of linen ever to emerge from a costume drama.

Jennifer Ehle and Colin Firth starred in *Pride and Prejudice* (1995).

OCTOBER

PUBLICATION OF
SENSE AND SENSIBILITY

Sense and Sensibility, Jane Austen's first published novel, came out in October 1811. It was published anonymously; the title page simply stated that it was 'By a Lady'.

Jane originally drafted the story in 1795 while living in Steventon, at which time it was called *Elinor & Marianne*. She revised the text in 1797–8, and then again after moving to Chawton in 1809–10.

Jane's brother Henry secured her a publisher: Thomas Egerton, who ran a military library in Whitehall. Egerton published *Sense and Sensibility* on commission, meaning that Jane took the financial risk rather than the publisher.

The first print run, which probably consisted of between 750–1,000 copies, completely sold out within two years, making Jane a handsome profit of £140.

The first advertisement for *Sense and Sensibility* appeared in *The Morning Chronicle* on 31 October 1811. It read:

In 3 vols. price 15s. in boards, a New Novel, called
SENSE and SENSIBILITY.
By Lady ___
Published by T. Egerton, Whitehall; and may be had at every Bookseller in the United Kingdom.

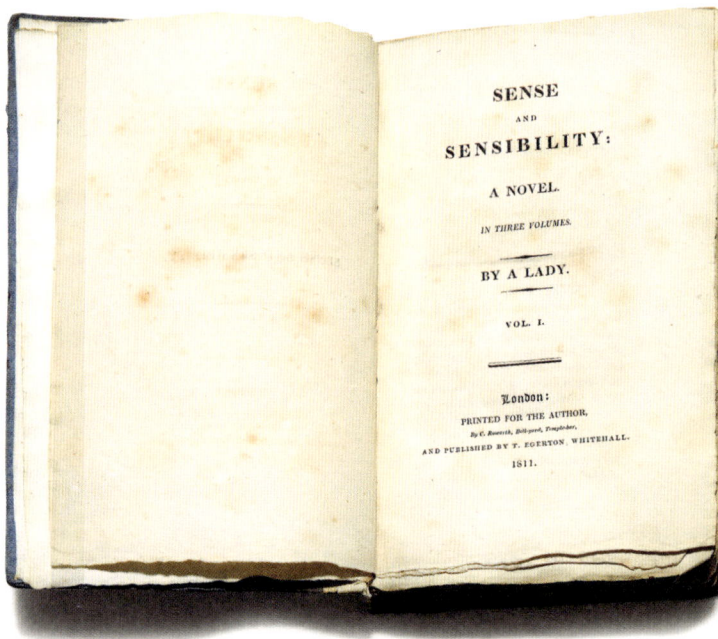

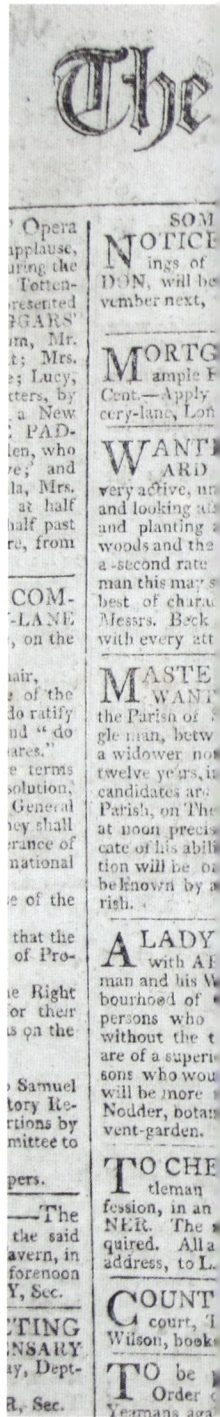

Morning Chronicle.

LONDON, THURSDAY, OCTOBER 31, 1811. [PRICE SIX-PENCE HALFPENNY.

E, 31ST OCTOBER, 1811.
en, that the Weekly Meet-
of ANTIQUARIES of LON-
ursday evening, the 7th of No-

CHOLAS CARLISLE, Sec.

NTED, on the Security of
the Sum of 20,000l. at Five per
Mr. Hanson, solicitor, Chan-

TION as LAND STEW-
AICLIFF, a middle-aged man,
and selling all sorts of stock,
workmen; understands draining
on waste lands; understands
all sorts of measures of work;
l, any lady, nobleman or gentle-
ery industrious servant with the
addressed for A. B. post-paid,
men, No. 67, Strand, will meet

WORKHOUSE.—
R for the WORKHOUSE of
out Cripplegate, London, a sin-
d forty-five years of age, and if
han one child, under the age of
. Persons desirous of becoming
end at the Workhouse of the said
ovember next, at twelve o'clock
rson then to produce a certifi-
grity and humanity. The elec-
uber.—Further particulars may
Overseers of the Poor of the Pa-

lity wishes to accommodate
and BOARD an elderly Gentle-
es. Her House is in the neigh-
Bedford Squares, and will suit
nforts of convenient Lodgings,
keeping. As the accommodations
terms are expected; but to per-
ame sleeping room, the charges
cards of address apply to Mrs.
d stationer, Tavistock-street, Co-

DRUGGISTS.—A Gen-
shed Business in the above Pro-
, wishes to meet with a PART-
references will be given and re-
be by letter, with real name and
e-house.

ES to be LET, in Copthal-
.—Apply for particulars of Mr.
ornhill.

RE-SOLD, pursuant to an
t of Chancery, made in a cause

VICTUALLING OFFICE, Oct. 29, 1811.

THE Commissioners for Victualling his Majesty's Navy do hereby give Notice,

That on Tuesday, the 19th November next, they will be ready so receive Tenders in writing (sealed up) and treat for Five Hundred Tons of OATMEAL, to be delivered at the Ports and in the proportions undermentioned, viz.—

Deptford	250 Tons
Portsmouth	180
Plymouth	70
	500 Tons.

One half thereof in one month, from the date of the contract, and the other half in one month afterwards; and to be paid for by Bills, payable with Interest, Ninety Days after date.
The Conditions of the Contract may be seen at the Secretary's Office.
No regard will be had to any tender in which the Price shall not be inserted in words at length, or that shall not be delivered to the Board before One o'clock on the said Tuesday the 19th of November next, nor unless the Person who makes the Tender, or some person on his behalf, attends, to answer when called for.

VICTUALLING-OFFICE, Oct. 29, 1811.

THE Commissioners for Victualling his Majesty's Navy, do hereby give Notice,

That on Friday the 15th November next, they will be ready to receive Tenders in writing (sealed up) and treat for Four Hundred Thousand Gallons of WEST INDIA RUM, to be delivered at the Ports and in the proportions undermentioned, viz.—

Plymouth	300,000 Gallons
Cork	100,000
	400,000 Gallons

One half thereof in the course of one month from the date of the contract, and the other half in one month afterwards; and to be paid for by bills payable, with interest, ninety days after date.
The conditions of the Contract may be seen at the Secretary's Office.
No regard will be had to any Tender in which the price shall not be inserted in words at length, or that shall not be delivered to the Board, before one o'clock on the said Friday the 15th November next; nor unless the person who makes the Tender, or some person on his behalf, attends to answer when called for.

TRANSPORT OFFICE, Oct. 18, 1811.

THE Commissioners for conducting his Majesty's Transport Service, for taking Care of Sick and Wounded Seamen, and for the Care and Custody of Prisoners of War, do hereby give notice,

That they will be ready at this Office, on Tuesday the 19th November, 1811, to receive sealed Tenders, and treat with such Persons as may be willing to Contract for Supplying MUSCOVADO SUGAR, CAROLINA RICE, PEARL BARLEY, and SAGO, for six months certain, from the 15th January 1812.
No Tender will be received after one o'clock on the day of Treaty, nor any noticed unless the Party, or an Agent for him, personally attend. Each Tender must be accompanied by a letter from two respectable Persons, engaging to become bound with the Person tendering, in the sum of 500l. for the due performance of the contract.
Farther particulars may be known by applying at this Office.

NAVY OFFICE, July 8, 1811.

BOOKS PUBLISHED THIS DAY.

TROTTER'S MEMOIRS of FOX.—The NEW EDITION is ready this day, accompanied by a POSTSCRIPT, containing some New Facts, and a Reply to the Animadversions of Party Writers. Price 14s. as before.
The P. S. may be had alone, price six-pence.
20, Paternoster-row, Oct. 28.

SUPPRESSED NEW NOVEL.

BRIGHTON in an UPROAR, &c. &c. &c.—A Novel founded on facts. By H. M. MORIARTY.
The above Work, comprising anecdotes of modern characters, was advertised to be published in August last, but was stopped from the Bookseller being threatened with a criminal prosecution.—The Authoress, therefore informs the Public that she has a few copies which may be had by applying to her at No. 29, Villiers-street, Strand.—Two vols. price 12s.
H. M. MORIARTY.

By T. EGERTON, Military Library, Whitehall.
In 1 vol. 8vo. price 12s. in boards, the Third Edition, with considerable additions, of

ELIOT'S TREATISE on the DEFENCE of PORTUGAL, and an Account of the Campaigns under Lord Viscount Wellington, from August, 1808, to the Battle of Albuera in 1811.
Illustrated with a large Map and six plates, of the Battles of Vimiera, Talavera, Busaco, Albuera, &c. &c. &c.

In 3 vols. price 15s. in boards, a New Novel, called

SENSE and SENSIBILITY. By Lady ——
Published by T. Egerton, Whitehall; and may be had of every Bookseller in the United Kingdom.

FRENCH REVOLUTION.

In 3 vols. 8vo. price 1l. 10s. in boards,

A COMPARATIVE DISPLAY of the DIFFERENT OPINIONS of the MOST DISTINGUISHED BRITISH WRITERS on the SUBJECT of the FRENCH REVOLUTION; followed by a Review and Comparison with Events. In this work will be found the Opinions of the late Mr. Fox, Mr. Burke, Lord Erskine, &c. &c. &c.
Printed for Thos. Egerton, Whitehall; and may be had of all Booksellers.

In 1 vol. 8vo. embellished with a Portrait, price 9s.

MEMOIRS of the LIFE of PRINCE POTEMKIN, Field Marshal in the Service of Russia; during the Reign of the Empress Catharine. From authentic documents, containing numerous Anecdotes, &c. hitherto unpublished.
Printed for, and sold by H. Colburn, Public Library, 50, Conduit-street; Anderson, Edinburgh; and Cumming, Dublin. Of whom and all Booksellers may be had, lately published, the 2d edition, in 1 vol. 8vo. embellished with a Portrait, price 10s. 6d. MEMOIRS of PRINCE EUGENE of SAVOY. Written by himself. For an account of this interesting work, see the Edinburgh Review, No. 33.

MAD. DE STAEL'S WORK ON LITERATURE, WITH MEMOIRS OF HER LIFE, &c.

In a few days will be published, in 2 vols. small octavo price 14s.

DE LA LITTERATURE, ANCIENNE et MODERNE. Par MADAME DE STAEL HOL-

'We have been exceedingly busy ever since you went away. In the first place we have had to rejoice two or three times every day at your having such very delightful weather for the whole of your Journey—& in the second place we have been obliged to take advantage of the delightful weather ourselves by going to see almost all our Neighbours.'

JANE TO CASSANDRA,
SATURDAY 25 OCTOBER 1800

'I am very glad the
new Cook begins so
well. Good apple
pies are a considerable
part of our domestic
happiness.'

JANE TO CASSANDRA,
TUESDAY 17 OCTOBER 1815

THE BATTLE OF TRAFALGAR

The Battle of Trafalgar was a naval battle that took place on 21 October 1805 between the British Royal Navy and the combined French and Spanish fleets. It was a decisive engagement and has become one of the most famous battles of the Napoleonic Wars.

The battle took place in the Atlantic Ocean, off Cape Trafalgar. The British fleet, led by Admiral Lord Nelson, was outnumbered by 33 allied ships to the British 27. In a bold move to address this imbalance, Nelson sailed his fleet directly at the enemy's flank, splitting it into three. The ensuing battle was fierce but the British were victorious, taking 20 allied ships and losing none.

The victory confirmed British naval supremacy, but it came at a price. The leading British ships were exposed to intense fire and Nelson's own ship, *Victory*, was almost knocked out of action. Nelson himself was shot during the battle and died shortly before it ended. Both Frank and Charles Austen were serving in the Royal Navy in 1805, but neither saw action at Trafalgar. Charles had been made commander in 1804 and was patrolling the Eastern seaboard of North America at the time. Frank came closer – he was serving as flag captain aboard HMS *Canopus*, based in the Mediterranean, and took part in Nelson's chase of the French fleet to the West Indies, but he was then sent to Gibraltar to collect provisions and was absent when the battle took place, which was of lifelong disappointment to him.

On 27 October Frank wrote to his wife Mary:

'As a national benefit I cannot but rejoice that our arms have been once again successful, but at the same time I cannot help feeling how very unfortunate we have been to be away at such a moment, and, by a fatal combination of unfortunate though unavoidable events, to lose all share in the glory of a day which surpasses all which ever went before, is what I cannot think of with any degree of patience.'

164

The Battle of Trafalgar, 21 October 1805, by Thomas Luny (1759–1837).

NIECES AND NEPHEWS

Jane Austen was a popular and beloved aunt to over 30 nieces and nephews. She and Cassandra spent a lot of time with their young relatives, who came to stay with them in Chawton and whom they visited in their own homes.

In October 1815 Jane wrote to her 10-year-old niece Caroline on the subject:

'Now that you are become an Aunt, you are a person of some consequence & must excite great Interest whatever You do. I have always maintained the importance of Aunts as much as possible, & I am sure of your doing the same now.— Beleive me my dear Sister-Aunt.'

CUP AND BALL

The cup and ball game, also known as 'Bilbocatch', was a popular Georgian pastime. The idea was to swing the ball on the string and catch it on the cup ('on the point'). This one belonged to the Knight family and Jane is believed to have played it while staying at Godmersham. She was exceptionally good at it, as her nephew James Edward Austen-Leigh noted in his book, *A Memoir of Jane Austen*:

'Her performances with cup-and-ball were marvellous. The one used at Chawton was an easy one, and she has been known to catch it on the point above an hundred times in succession, till her hand was weary.'

JANE AUSTEN AROUND THE WORLD

The Jane Austen Society of North America (JASNA) was founded in 1979 by Joan Austen-Leigh, Henry G. Burke and J. David Grey. An inaugural dinner was held on 5 October at the Gramercy Park Hotel in Manhattan, a glamorous occasion attended by 100 founding members.

Since then, the society's ranks have grown to more than 5,000, making JASNA the largest literary society devoted to Jane Austen in the world. They meet for an Annual General Meeting every October in a different state, celebrating all things Austen with talks, workshops, performances, food, drink, conversation, dresses and dancing.

Other societies dedicated to Jane Austen's life and works now also flourish around the world, from Australia and New Zealand to Argentina, Brazil, Spain, Italy, Japan and Iceland. Jane Austen's novels have been translated into many languages, and adaptations set in other countries and time periods show how universal her plots and themes are.

Aishwarya Rai and Martin Henderson starred in *Bride and Prejudice* (2004), which transposed the story of *Pride and Prejudice* to modern-day India, in a riot of colour and Bollywood-style singing and dancing.

'We have got the 2^{d} vol. of Espriella's Letters, & I read it aloud by candlelight.'

171

JANE TO CASSANDRA,
SATURDAY 1 OCTOBER 1808

NOVEMBER

'How could you have a
wet day on Thursday?—
with us it was a Prince
of days, the most
delightful we have had
for weeks, soft, bright,
with a brisk wind from
the South west;—
everybody was out &
talking of spring—
& Martha & I did not
know how to turn back.'

JANE TO CASSANDRA,
SUNDAY 20 NOVEMBER 1808

—
174

KEEPING WARM

By November, the days are short and the weather cold. The house in Chawton has a fireplace in every room, but it is unlikely they would all have been lit at once. Instead, the Austen women would have sat together in the evenings to save on fuel and candles. Regency dresses were notoriously flimsy, but hidden underneath there would have been layers of warm petticoats and stockings, with a cosy shawl over the top.

In November 1812 Jane wrote to Martha Lloyd about just such a present for their neighbour, Miss Benn:

'Cassandra & I think that something of the Shawl kind to wear over her Shoulders within doors in very cold weather might be useful, but it must not be very handsome or she would not use it. Her long Fur tippet is almost worn out.'

Men's clothing was more suitable for cold weather. In *Sense and Sensibility*, Colonel Brandon 'sought the constitutional safeguard of a flannel waistcoat' to guard against chills, while in *Northanger Abbey*, Henry Tilney is 'booted and greatcoated' for his journey to Woodston. Even so, some people will always sacrifice comfort for fashion: in *Northanger Abbey* Mrs Allen hopes that her husband will wear his greatcoat on a rainy day in Bath, though she knows he will not as 'he had rather do anything in the world than walk out in a greatcoat'.

'Upon my word, this is charming to be standing about among such friends! And such a noble fire!—I am quite roasted.'

EMMA, VOLUME III, CHAPTER 2

Illustration by Hugh Thomson for *Pride and Prejudice* (MacMillan & Co, 1894).

AN AUTUMN WALK

OPPOSITE The lane to Steventon church. The Austens would have known this route well – the Reverend George Austen was Rector of Steventon and the family worshipped there every Sunday.

Persuasion is a distinctly autumnal novel. One pivotal scene takes place on 'a very fine November day', when the characters go for a walk in the fields near Uppercross. Captain Wentworth and Louisa Musgrove go off by themselves and Anne painfully overhears them talking about her on the other side of a hedge.

Just as they were setting off, the gentlemen returned. They had taken out a young dog, who had spoilt their sport, and sent them back early. Their time and strength, and spirits, were, therefore, exactly ready for this walk, and they entered into it with pleasure. Could Anne have foreseen such a junction, she would have staid at home; but, from some feelings of interest and curiosity, she fancied now that it was too late to retract, and the whole six set forward together in the direction chosen by the Miss Musgroves, who evidently considered the walk as under their guidance.

Anne's object was, not to be in the way of anybody; and where the narrow paths across the fields made many separations necessary, to keep with her brother and sister. Her pleasure in the walk must arise from the exercise and the day, from the view of the last smiles of the year upon the tawny leaves, and withered hedges, and from repeating to herself some few of the thousand poetical descriptions extant of autumn, that season of peculiar and inexhaustible influence on the mind of taste and tenderness, that season which had drawn from every poet, worthy of being read, some attempt at description, or some lines of feeling. She occupied her mind as much as possible in such like musings and quotations; but it was not possible, that when within reach of Captain Wentworth's conversation with either of the Miss Musgroves, she should not try to hear it; yet she

caught little very remarkable. It was mere lively chat, such as any young persons, on an intimate footing, might fall into. He was more engaged with Louisa than with Henrietta. Louisa certainly put more forward for his notice than her sister. This distinction appeared to increase, and there was one speech of Louisa's which struck her. After one of the many praises of the day, which were continually bursting forth, Captain Wentworth added:--

'What glorious weather for the Admiral and my sister! They meant to take a long drive this morning; perhaps we may hail them from some of these hills. They talked of coming into this side of the country. I wonder whereabouts they will upset to-day. Oh! it does happen very often, I assure you; but my sister makes nothing of it; she would as lieve be tossed out as not.'

'Ah! You make the most of it, I know,' cried Louisa, 'but if it were really so, I should do just the same in her place. If I loved a man, as she loves the Admiral, I would always be with him, nothing should ever separate us, and I would rather be overturned by him, than driven safely by anybody else.'

It was spoken with enthusiasm.

'Had you?' cried he, catching the same tone; 'I honour you!' And there was silence between them for a little while.

PERSUASION, VOLUME I, CHAPTER 10

I am very much obliged to you, my dear Anna, & should be very happy to come & see you again if I could, but I have not a day disengaged. We are expecting your Uncle Charles tomorrow; and I am to go the next day to Hanwell to fetch some Miss Moores who are to stay here till Saturday; then comes Sunday & Eliz^{th} Gibson, and on Monday Your Uncle Henry takes us both to Chawton. It is therefore really impossible, but I am very much obliged to You & to Mr B. Lefroy for wishing it. We should find plenty to say, no doubt, & I should like to hear Charlotte Dewar's Letter; however, though I do not hear it, I am glad she has written to you. I like first Cousins to be first Cousins, & interested about each other. They are but one remove from B^r & S^r–

We all came away very much pleased with our visit I assure You. We talked of you for about a mile & a half with great satisfaction, & I have been just sending a very good account of you to Miss Beckford, with a description of your Dress for Susan & Maria.–Your Uncle & Edwd left us this morning. The hopes of the Former in his Cause, do not lessen.–We were all at the Play last night, to see Miss O'neal in Isabella. I do not think she was quite equal to my expectation. I fancy I want something more than can be. Acting seldom satisfies me. I took two Pocket handkerchiefs, but had very little occasion for either. She is an elegant creature however & hugs Mr Younge delightfully.–

I am very much obliged to you, my
dear Anna, I should bee very happy to
come & see you again if I could, but
have not a day disengaged. We are ex:
pecting your Uncle Charles tomorrow;
and I am to go the next day to Hamwell
to fetch some Miss Moores who are to
stay here till Saturday; then comes
Sunday & Eliz.th Gibson, and on Monday
your Uncle Henry takes us both to
Hanwton. It is therefore really impos:
sible, but I am very much obliged to
you & to Mr. B. Lefroy for wishing it.
You should find plenty to say, no doubt,

THE NETHERFIELD BALL

In Pride and Prejudice, *the Netherfield Ball takes place on 26 November – as Mr Bingley recollects when he sees Lizzy again at Pemberley. The ball is significant for many reasons, not least because it is the first time that Lizzy dances with Mr Darcy.*

She danced next with an officer, and had the refreshment of talking of Wickham, and of hearing that he was universally liked. When those dances were over, she returned to Charlotte Lucas, and was in conversation with her, when she found herself suddenly addressed by Mr. Darcy who took her so much by surprise in his application for her hand, that, without knowing what she did, she accepted him. He walked away again immediately, and she was left to fret over her own want of presence of mind; Charlotte tried to console her:

'I dare say you will find him very agreeable.'

'Heaven forbid! *That* would be the greatest misfortune of all! To find a man agreeable whom one is determined to hate! Do not wish me such an evil.'

When the dancing recommenced, however, and Darcy approached to claim her hand, Charlotte could not help cautioning her in a whisper, not to be a simpleton, and allow her fancy for Wickham to make her appear unpleasant in the eyes of a man ten times his consequence. Elizabeth made no answer, and took her place in the set, amazed at the dignity to which she was arrived in being allowed to stand opposite to Mr. Darcy, and reading in her neighbours' looks, their equal amazement in beholding it. They stood for some time without speaking a word; and she began to imagine that their silence was to last through the two dances, and at first was resolved not to break it; till suddenly fancying that it would be the greater punishment to her partner to oblige him to talk, she made some slight observation on the dance. He replied, and was again silent. After a pause of some minutes, she addressed him a second time with:– 'It is *your* turn to say something now, Mr. Darcy. *I* talked about the dance, and *you* ought to make some sort of remark on the size of the room, or the number of couples.'

He smiled, and assured her that whatever she wished him to say should be said.

'Very well. That reply will do for the present. Perhaps by and by I may observe that private balls are much pleasanter than public ones. But *now* we may be silent.'

'Do you talk by rule, then, while you are dancing?'

'Sometimes. One must speak a little, you know. It would look odd to be entirely silent for half an hour together; and yet for the advantage of *some*, conversation ought to be so arranged, as that they may have the trouble of saying as little as possible.'

***PRIDE AND PREJUDICE*, VOLUME I, CHAPTER 18**

DANCING SLIPPERS

These white satin slippers belonged to Jane's niece, Marianne Knight. Both men and women would wear slippers like this to a ball – changing into them from their street shoes or boots once they had arrived at the ballroom.

These slippers are made of fine silk with thin leather soles, and silk ribbons to keep them on. With their square toes, they were not designed to fit the right or left foot, as modern shoes are, instead they were interchangeable.

Dancing slippers were incredibly fragile and wore out quickly, sometimes only lasting for a single ball before the delicate fabrics disintegrated. This well-preserved pair does not appear to have been worn.

WHITE SOUP

White soup was an elegant dish made of a meat broth, cream and ground almonds, that would have been served as part of the supper at private balls. Served around midnight, this late meal would give the party the energy to continue dancing until the small hours.

Mr Bingley famously mentions white soup in *Pride and Prejudice*, when planning his own ball at Netherfield:

'...as for the ball, it is quite a settled thing; and as soon as Nicholls has made white soup enough, I shall send round my cards.'

PRIDE AND PREJUDICE,
VOLUME I, CHAPTER 11

DECEMBER

GILBERT WHITE

On 16 December 1775 the Hampshire naturalist Gilbert White recorded the weather in his diary as, 'fog, sun, sweet day.' We can imagine the Austen boys running in the fields, their breath sending out clouds of mist into the cold air, while back at home their mother went into labour with their baby sister.

JANE AUSTEN'S BIRTH

Jane Austen was born on the evening of Saturday 16 December 1775 at Steventon Rectory. She was the Austens' seventh child, and the second girl. Reverend Austen wrote proudly to Mrs Susanna Walter, his half sister-in-law, the following day:

'You have doubtless been for some time in expectation of hearing from Hampshire, and perhaps wondered a little we were in our old age grown such bad reckoners but so it was, for Cassy certainly expected to have been brought to bed a month ago: however last night the time came, and without a great deal of warning, everything was soon happily over. We have now another girl, a present plaything for her sister Cassy and a future companion. She is to be Jenny.'

Jane was baptised at home by her father, like all the Austen children. Her christening in Steventon church would not take place until April the following year.

The weather was bitterly cold and snow fell thickly. Mrs Austen stayed in bed with her baby warmly swaddled against the cold, while downstairs the maids were kept busy washing, cooking and stoking the fires and the laundry woman trudged up from the village to wash the extra sheets, baby napkins and clothes.

FAMILY THEATRICALS

In the winter of 1787, when Jane turned 12, the Austen children staged a series of plays in the barn behind the house. James, the eldest, had recently returned from a trip to France and was wild about theatricals, which were a fashionable pastime.

The plays they performed were comedies, including *Bon Ton*, *The Wonder* and *High Life Below Stairs*. Their cousin Eliza took the leading roles, flirting and showing off. James, smitten with his glamorous cousin, wrote a prologue and epilogue for her to speak in *The Wonder*.

Jane may have acted too. One of the plays performed was Fielding's satire *Tom Thumb*. The diminutive hero was often played by a child, so it is possible that Jane took on the role. If not, she was certainly watching with glowing eyes fixed on the stage, a life-long love of theatre beginning to take root.

Jane was also writing her own stories and sketches at this time, including an extraordinary short play entitled *The Mystery, an Unfinished Comedy*. Later, in *Mansfield Park*, she wrote about amateur theatricals, displaying her understanding of all the glamour and allure of play-acting:

'Happily for him, a love of the theatre is so general, an itch for acting so strong among young people, that he could hardly out-talk the interest of his hearers. From the first casting of the parts to the epilogue it was all bewitching, and there were few who did not wish to have been a party concerned, or would have hesitated to try their skill.'

MANSFIELD PARK,
VOLUME I, CHAPTER 13

— 193

Illustration by Hugh Thomson for
Mansfield Park (MacMillan & Co, 1897).

A CHRISTMAS VISIT

In Emma, *Mr Woodhouse is persuaded to travel to Randalls for dinner on Christmas Eve. On the way, Emma finds herself closeted in a carriage with a sprightly Mr Elton and her dour brother-in-law, Mr John Knightley.*

'What an excellent device,' said he, 'the use of a sheepskin for carriages. How very comfortable they make it;—impossible to feel cold with such precautions. The contrivances of modern days indeed have rendered a gentleman's carriage perfectly complete. One is so fenced and guarded from the weather, that not a breath of air can find its way unpermitted. Weather becomes absolutely of no consequence. It is a very cold afternoon—but in this carriage we know nothing of the matter.—Ha! snows a little I see.'

'Yes,' said John Knightley, 'and I think we shall have a good deal of it.'

'Christmas weather,' observed Mr. Elton. 'Quite seasonable; and extremely fortunate we may think ourselves that it did not begin yesterday, and prevent this day's party, which it might very possibly have done, for Mr. Woodhouse would hardly have ventured had there been much snow on the ground; but now it is of no consequence. This is quite the season indeed for friendly meetings. At Christmas every body invites their friends about them, and people think little of even the worst weather. I was snowed up at a friend's house once for a week. Nothing could be pleasanter. I went for only one night, and could not get away till that very day se'nnight.'

Mr. John Knightley looked as if he did not comprehend the pleasure, but said only, coolly,

'I cannot wish to be snowed up a week at Randalls.'

At another time Emma might have been amused, but she was too much astonished now at Mr. Elton's spirits for other feelings. Harriet seemed quite forgotten in the expectation of a pleasant party.

'We are sure of excellent fires,' continued he, 'and every thing in the greatest comfort. Charming people, Mr. and Mrs. Weston;—Mrs. Weston indeed is much beyond praise, and he is exactly what one values, so hospitable, and so fond of society;—it will be a small party, but where small parties are select, they are perhaps the most agreeable of any. Mr. Weston's dining-room does not accommodate more than ten comfortably; and for my part, I would rather, under such circumstances, fall short by two than exceed by two. I think you will agree with me, (turning with a soft air to Emma,) I think I shall certainly have your approbation, though Mr. Knightley perhaps, from being used to the large parties of London, may not quite enter into our feelings.'

'I know nothing of the large parties of London, sir—I never dine with any body.'

'Indeed! (in a tone of wonder and pity,) I had no idea that the law had been so great a slavery. Well, sir, the time must come when you will be paid for all this, when you will have little labour and great enjoyment.'

'My first enjoyment,' replied John Knightley, as they passed through the sweep-gate, 'will be to find myself safe at Hartfield again.'

EMMA, VOLUME I, CHAPTER 13

MINCE PIES

Mince pies were a Christmas staple during the Regency period, just as they are today. Their origin can be traced back to the thirteenth century and they are filled with tradition and symbolism. Eating a mince pie every day of the 12 days of Christmas was said to bring 12 months of happiness in the new year.

The mincemeat filling includes cinnamon, cloves and nutmeg to represent the gifts of the Magi to the baby Jesus, and tradition says that it should be stirred clockwise to bring good luck for the coming year. The pies are often topped with a pastry star to represent the star of Bethlehem.

Early mince pie recipes included meat as the main ingredient – usually beef, mutton or venison – but as time went on it was removed. Martha Lloyd's recipe for mince pies is light and modern, with lemon and apple adding freshness to the rich filling.

Lemon Mince Pies

Take a good lemon, squeeze out the juice. Boil the pulp with the rind tender, and pound it very fine. Put to it three quarters of a pound of currants, half a pound of sugar, half an ounce of orange flower water, a good glass of Mountain or Brandy. Put in your juice with half a nutmeg, a little mace, citron or candied orange peel as you please. You must put three quarter of a pound of beef suet chopped very fine and mixed with the currants. Half a dozen apples chopped fine and added to it is a great improvement.

'I am sorry to say that I could not eat a Mincepie at Mr Papillon's; I was rather head-achey that day, & c^d not venture on anything sweet except Jelly; but that was excellent.'

JANE TO CASSANDRA,
FRIDAY 29 JANUARY 1813

197

that I feel it right to assure you of my not
having forgotten your kind recommendation
of an early copy for C. H. — & that I have
W. Murray's promise of its being sent to
HRH. under cover to you, three days previous
to the Work being really out. —

I must make use of this opportunity to thank you
dear Sir, for the very high praise you bestow on my other
Novels — . I am too vain to wish to convince you that
you have praised them beyond their Merit. —

My greatest anxiety at present is that this 4th. work
shd. not disgrace what was good in the others. But
on this point I will do myself the justice to declare
that whatever may be my wishes for its success,
I am very strongly haunted by the idea that to
those Readers who have preferred P&P. it will appear
inferior in Wit, & to those who have preferred MP.
very inferior in good Sense. Such as it is
however, I hope you will do me the favour of
accepting a Copy. Mr. M. will have directions
for sending one. I am quite honoured by your

JANE AUSTEN TO REVEREND JAMES STANIER CLARKE, MONDAY 11 DECEMBER 1815

Dec: 11.

Dear Sir

My Emma is now so near publication that I feel it right to assure You of my not having forgotten your kind recommendation of an early Copy for Cⁿ H.–& that I have Mr Murray's promise of its being sent to HRH. under cover to You, three days previous to the Work being really out.–

I must make use of this opportunity to thank you dear Sir, for the very high praise you bestow on my other Novels–I am too vain to wish to convince you that you have praised them beyond their Merit.–

My greatest anxiety at present is that this 4th work shd not disgrace what was good in the others. But on this point I will do myself the justice to declare that whatever may be my wishes for its' success, I am very strongly haunted by the idea that to those Readers who have preferred P&P. it will appear inferior in Wit, & to those who have preferred MP. very inferior in good Sense. Such as it is however, I hope you will do me the favour of accepting a Copy. Mr M. will have directions for sending one. I am quite honoured by your thinking me capable of drawing such a Clergyman as you gave the sketch of in your note of Nov: 16. But I assure you I am <u>not</u>. The comic part of the Character I might be equal to, but not the Good, the Enthusiastic, the Literary. Such a Man's Conversation must at times be on subjects of Science & Philosophy of which I know nothing–or at least be occasionally abundant in quotations & allusions which a Woman, who like me, knows only her own Mother-tongue & has read very little in that, would be totally without the power of giving.–A Classical Education, or at any rate, a very extensive acquaintance with English Literature, Ancient & Modern, appears to me quite Indispensable for the person who wd do any justice to your Clergyman–And I think I may boast myself to be, with all possible Vanity, the most unlearned, & uninformed Female who ever dared to be an Authoress.

beleive me, dear Sir,
Your obligd & faithl Hum. Servt.
J.A.

A MEMOIR OF JANE AUSTEN

Jane's nephew James Edward Austen-Leigh published his biography of his aunt, *A Memoir of Jane Austen*, in December 1869. It was the first full-length biography of Jane Austen and the only one written by someone she knew.

The *Memoir* brought together James Edward's own recollections of his aunt and those of his sister Caroline and their half-sister Anna Lefroy as well as their cousin, Cassy Esten Austen.

While the *Memoir*'s cosy Victorian portrayal of Jane Austen has been challenged by later biographers, it was an important work, introducing the public to Jane's works and generating popular interest in her novels, which until then had only been read by the literary elite. It remained the most important biographical work on Jane Austen for over half a century.

A Memoir of Jane Austen, by James Edward Austen-Leigh. First edition (1870).

JANE AUSTEN.

LONDON: RICHARD BENTLEY, 1870.

A MEMOIR

OF

JANE AUSTEN

BY

HER NEPHEW

J. E. AUSTEN-LEIGH

VICAR OF BRAY, BERKS

FIDE·ET·FIDUCIA

LONDON

RICHARD BENTLEY, NEW BURLINGTON STREET

Publisher in Ordinary to Her Majesty

1870

'Immediately surrounding Mrs Musgrove were the little Harvilles, whom she was sedulously guarding from the tyranny of the two children from the Cottage, expressly arrived to amuse them. On one side was a table occupied by some chattering girls, cutting up silk and gold paper; and on the other were tressels and trays, bending under the weight of brawn and cold pies, where riotous boys were holding high revel; the whole completed by a roaring Christmas fire, which seemed determined to be heard, in spite of all the noise of the others. Charles and Mary also came in, of course, during their visit, and Mr Musgrove made a point of paying his respects to Lady Russell, and sat down close to her for ten minutes, talking with a very raised voice, but from the clamour of the children on his knees, generally in vain. It was a fine family-piece.'

PERSUASION, VOLUME II, CHAPTER 2

INDEX

Images are indicated in **bold**.

apples 73, 162
Austen, Cassandra **31**, 38, 48, 117
Austen, Cassandra (mother) 51, 64, 112, 137, 191
Austen, Cassy Esten 200
Austen, Charles 88, 164
Austen, Edward 112
Austen, Frank 54, 164
Austen, George (father) 64, 80, 191
Austen, Henry 96, 158
Austen, James 55, 192
Austen, Jane
  birth 191
  death 117
Austen-Leigh, Caroline 200
Austen-Leigh, James Edward 55, 167, 200, **201**
Austen-Leigh, Joan 168
Austen-mania 155

Bath 80, **81**, 152, **153**
bees 38
Bennet, Elizabeth 40–1, 56–7, 66–7, 119, 155, 183
Bennet, Lydia 96, 142
Bigg, Alethea 20
Bigg, Catherine 134
Bigg-Wither, Harris 134
Box Hill 100, **101**

Bride and Prejudice (film) **169**
Brydges, Edward 130
Burke, Henry G. 168

cake 104
Carpenter, T. Edward 120
Chawton 7, 18, 112, 121, 206
cheese on toast 130–1
Christmas 194–6, 203
clothing 176
Clueless (film) **123**
Corder, Joan **96**
cup and ball game 167

dancing 16–17, 184
Darcy, Fitzwilliam 17, 40–1, 66–7, 155, 183
Darnell, Beatrix 91
Darnell, Dorothy 90–1
Davies, Andrew 155
de Feuillide, Comtesse (Eliza Hancock) 27, 34, 96, 192
Dress Up Day 121

Egerton, Thomas 18, 158
Ehle, Jennifer **154**, 155
Emma 71, 73, 94, 100, 123, 176, 194, 199
Engleheart, George **16**

films and television 122–3, **132**, **146**, **154**, 155, **169**, **182**

fireplaces 176
Firth, Colin **154**, 155
food 73, 104, 130–1, 162, **186**, 187, 196, **197**
Fowle, Tom 38, 48
French Revolution **26**

Gabell, Henry 87
games 167
gardening 50–1, 54, **128–9**
Garson, Greer **122**
Gibson, Mary 54
Godmersham 48, 54, 84, **118**, 167
Grey, J. David 168

Hancock, Eliza (Comtesse de Feuillide) 27, 34, 96, 192
Hancock, Philadelphia 34, **35**
Hancock, Tysoe Saul 34
handkerchiefs 134, **135**
harvest 150–1
Hassall, Joan **56**, **66**, **126**
Hastings, Warren 34
Heath, W. **143**
A History of England 48
holidays 142, **143**

Jane Austen Festival 152, **153**
Jane Austen Society 90–1, 120
Jane Austen Society of

North America (JASNA) 168
Jenkins, Elizabeth 91
Jerome, Helen 40–1
Johnson, Celia 40

Knight, Fanny **31**
Knight, Marianne 184
Knightley, Keira **182**

landscape gardening **128–9**
lavender 138–9
Lefroy, Anna **62–3**, 180, 200
Lefroy, Fanny Caroline 51
Lefroy, Tom **16**, 17
Leigh, Cassandra (mother) 51, 64, 112, 137, 191
Leigh, Thomas 137
lemon mince pies 196
letters
  to Anna Lefroy 180, **181**
  to Caroline Austen-Leigh 58, **59**
  to Cassandra 8, 17, 18, **22**, 23, **36**, 37, 42, 46, 48, 54, 78, **82**, 83, 84, 88, 99, 103, 104, 130, 144, 148, **148**, 151, 161–2, 171, 174, **197**
  destruction 55
  to Fanny Knight 31
  to Frank Austen 111, 114–15

to James Edward Austen-
  Leigh 87
to Martha Lloyd 18, 176
to niece Caroline 166
to Phila Walter 27
to Rev James Stanier
  Clarke 68, **69**, **198**, 199
Lloyd, Martha 18, 20, 54,
  112, 131, 196
Lloyd, Mary 137
London 14
Louis XVI **26**, 27
Luny, Thomas **165**
Lybbe-Powys, Tom 64
Lyme Regis 142, **144–5**

Mansfield Park 53, 55, 75,
  88, **126**, 127, 192–3
Manydown Park 134
*Martha Lloyd's Household
  Book* 20, 38, 131, 150
A Memoir of Jane Austen
  (Austen-Leigh) 55, 167,
  200, **201**
mince pies 196, **197**
Muller, John S. **102–3**
music 24, **25**

Netherfield Ball 183
nieces and nephews 166
Northanger Abbey 80, 176

ointments 38
Olivier, Laurence **122**
orange wine 20

patchwork 84, **85**
Pearson, Mary 96, **97**
Pemberley 119
Persuasion 33, 80, 81,
  132–3, 142, 179, 203
piano **25**
pies 162, **163**
Pike, Rosamund **182**
plays 39–40, 192–3
Pride and Prejudice 16–18,
  19, 23, 39–40, 56–7, 66–7,
  96, 119, 121, 122, 142, **154**,
  155, **176**, **182**, 183, 187

raspberry vinegar 150
recipes 20, 38, 131, 150, 196
Repton, Humphry 128–9
Root, Amanda **132**
roses 54, **106**, 107

salves 38
'scraps' 55
seaside 142, **143**
Sense and Sensibility 14,
  15, 18, 63, 112, 139, **146**,
  147, 158, **159**, 176
sewing 84, **85**, 135, 136, 176
Sheridan, Richard 18
Sieveking, Georg Heinrich
  26
Silverstone, Alicia **123**
slippers 184, **185**
Smart, John 34, **35**
societies 90–1, 120, 168
Sotherton 127

soup **186**, 187
Southampton 54
spring cleaning 42–3
stage productions 39–40
Steventon Rectory 18, 51,
  64
Stoneleigh Abbey **136**, 137

tea 46
theatre 39–40, 192–3
Thomson, Hugh **15**, **142**,
  176, **193**
toasted cheese 130–1
topaz crosses **88–9**
Trafalgar, Battle of 164, **165**

Uppercross 132–3

Vauxhall Gardens **102–3**

walking 179
Walter, Susanna 191
Watts, William **118**
weather 12, 58, 78, 111, 144,
  161, 174, 190
Wentworth, Captain 33
Whistler, Rex 40
White, Gilbert 12, 190
white soup **186**, 187
Winchester **86**, 87, **116**
Winslet, Kate **146**
Wise, Greg **146**
Wood, William **97**

ABOUT JANE AUSTEN'S HOUSE

'every body is acquainted with Chawton & speaks of it as a remarkably pretty village, & every body knows the House we describe–but nobody fixes on the right.'
Jane to Cassandra, 9 December 1808

Here, in this inspiring Hampshire cottage, Jane Austen lived for the last eight years of her life, from July 1809 until May 1817. Here her genius flourished, and she wrote or revised and had published her six great novels: *Sense and Sensibility*, *Pride and Prejudice*, *Mansfield Park*, *Emma*, *Northanger Abbey* and *Persuasion*.

This house is crucial to the story of these extraordinary works, and to Jane Austen's life as a writer. To her, it was more than just a house – it was a place of refuge, security and inspiration, where she finally had the space and time in which to write.

But while Jane Austen moved here in 1809, the story of this remarkable house began long before. Originally built as a thatched, timber dwelling in the late fifteenth or early sixteenth century, it was first used as a farmhouse and then as a coaching inn. In the eighteenth century it became part of the Knight family estate, owned by distant relatives of the Austens, and it was eventually inherited by Jane's brother Edward.

Jane Austen left Chawton in May 1817 to seek medical treatment in Winchester. She died two months later, on 18 July 1817, and was buried in Winchester Cathedral.

Today, Jane Austen's House is a Grade I listed building, an accredited museum, and one of the most important literary sites in the world. It holds an unparalleled collection of Austen treasures, including Jane's personal letters and first editions of her novels, items of jewellery that she cherished, portraits of her friends and family, and the tiny writing table at which she wrote.

But more than this – the house quietly evokes the atmosphere of Austen's world. The gentle sound of piano music drifts from the drawing room, the buzz of quiet conversation creeps down from the bedroom. The chiming of the grandfather clock and the creak of footsteps on the historic floorboards all add to the charm and atmosphere of this special place.

Visitors wander from room to room, following in Jane's footsteps as they explore the house where she lived and wrote, discovering objects and stories that inspired her, and learning about her writing life.

We are privileged to look after Jane's beloved Chawton home, and to welcome visitors from around the world who love Jane Austen's works as much as we do.

This book is just one of the ways in which we hope to share Jane's extraordinary home with the world. Every copy sold supports our work. Thank you for being part of the story!

PICTURE CREDITS

First published in the United Kingdom
in 2025 by
Pitkin
43 Great Ormond Street
London
WC1N 3HZ

An imprint of B. T. Batsford Holdings Limited

ISBN 978 1 84994 904 0

A CIP catalogue record for this book is available from the
British Library.

10 9 8 7 6 5 4 3 2

Reproduction by Rival Colour Ltd, UK
Printed by Elma Basim, Turkey

This book can be ordered direct from the publisher at
www.batsfordbooks.com, or try your local bookshop.

Distributed throughout the UK and Europe by Abrams &
Chronicle Books, 1 West Smithfield, London EC1A 9JU
and 57 rue Gaston Tessier, 75166 Paris, France

www.abramsandchronicle.co.uk
info@abramsandchronicle.co.uk

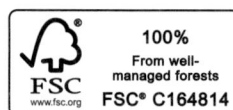

FSC
www.fsc.org
100%
From well-
managed forests
FSC® C164814